What
Car Dealers
Don't Want You to Know

What
Car Dealers
Don't Want You to Know

Mark Eskeldson

Technews Publishing
———
Fair Oaks, CA

Copyright © 2000 by Technews Corp.

The information contained in this book is true and complete to
the best of our knowledge. Strategies for negotiating vehicle
purchases and leases are suggested as ones that have been successful in the past, but results may vary. No liability is assumed with respect to the use of the information herein.

Library of Congress Catalog Card Number: 00-191512

ISBN: 0-9640560-7-0

Published by
Technews Publishing, a division of Technews Corp.,
7840 Madison Avenue, Suite 185, Fair Oaks, CA 95628

Third Edition
0 9 8 7 6 5 4 3 2 1
September, 2000

Manufactured in the United States of America.

Cover Design by Paula Schlosser

DEDICATION

This book is dedicated to the honest car dealers and sales-people across the country who are tired of the greedy ones giving their industry a bad name.

ABOUT THE AUTHOR

Mark Eskeldson is the author of *What Auto Mechanics Don't Want You to Know,* the first hard-hitting exposé of the biggest names in auto repair. He has been involved in the auto industry for over 21 years, including jobs at several new-car dealerships, and is certified by the National Institute for Automotive Service Excellence.

The author's books have been featured in *Kiplinger's, Smart Money, Reader's Digest, The Wall Street Journal,* and on ABC, NBC and CBS TV.

ACKNOWLEDGMENTS

This book would not have been possible without the help of many people. My special thanks to the following: the current and former car salesmen who disclosed "the tricks of the trade," the victims of dishonest salesmen who told me their stories, and the investigators and attorneys who have worked on consumer-fraud cases involving dealers.

Thanks also to James Bragg of Fighting Chance for providing information on vehicle prices, holdback and dealer incentives.

Contents

Introduction

A recent hidden-camera investigation by KCBS-TV caught 11 out of 14 new-car dealers lying, cheating and overcharging customers on new-car leases and purchases. I helped KCBS conduct their investigation, and the car dealers tried to keep it off the air. At least four dealers threatened to pull their advertising from the station, but KCBS aired the five-part series anyway. As a result of their investigation, hundreds of people received refunds and one dealer may now be facing criminal charges.

National surveys of consumer complaints continue to find car dealers making the top 10 list. (The last survey of complaints listed auto sales as #1 and auto leasing as #7.) And a number of car dealer investigations, including the recent one by KCBS, found scores of victims who had not filed complaints because they were not sure that they had been cheated.

No wonder so many people would rather have a root canal than negotiate with a car salesman! Consumers rate haggling with salespeople as the most unpleasant part of the whole car-buying experience. So, what's a person to do? Pay retail on the car you want (or buy a Saturn) just to avoid the hassle? Or is there an easy way for you to get a big discount on the car of your choice?

The answers to those questions (and many more) can be found inside this book. And no, you're not going to learn how to go nine rounds in a knock-down, drag-out negotiating battle with a salesman. (No one wants that, except the salesman.) Fortunately, that's not necessary. The secrets of car dealers will be revealed so your next car-buying adventure will be not only profitable, but fun.

You'll learn the best methods of getting great deals on new cars and trucks—including the best way to have someone else do the haggling for you, if that's what you want. And you'll learn how to find out the dealer's *real* cost on a new vehicle (it's often lower than the dealer invoice number), where to buy extended warranties at discount prices, plus the pros and cons of using the Internet to research and/or buy a car.

Did you know that many lease customers have been charged higher vehicle prices than they thought they were getting? Or that many have been charged undisclosed lease rates of 10% to 12% when car loans were only 8%? *No wonder dealers love leasing!* Mandatory disclosure of cap costs on leases started in 1998, but that doesn't mean that dealers stopped doing secret price hikes. They're still doing them, and they're still charging higher undisclosed lease rates.

To make sure you don't lose those big discounts that you'll be negotiating, I've exposed the most common tricks that dishonest dealers use to overcharge their customers. You'll learn all about leasing scams; disappearing down payments, rebates and trade-ins; secret price and interest rate hikes; payment packing; and how to calculate your own payments so you can tell when a dealer is trying to rip you off.

NOTE: The term "salesman" was used throughout this book to improve readability and was not intended as a slight to the female salespeople of the auto industry.

1

The Rip-offs Continue

In February of 1995, ABC's *PrimeTime Live* did a show on auto leasing titled, "The Best Deal?" A female reporter went undercover, with a hidden camera, to see what would happen to several female "buyers" when they went shopping for new cars. Their stories, along with video-taped conversations with salesmen, revealed outrageous attempts to mislead and overcharge on new-car leases.

Out of ten dealers that were visited, five tried to talk the shopper into leasing instead of buying. In trying to convince her not to buy, one salesman said, "It's coming to the point where people are not even buying cars anymore." Another salesman said, "See, we learned a long time ago you don't buy things that depreciate, you lease them." And a third salesman said (convincingly), "It's the cheapest way ever to drive an automobile, period."

So, what kind of leasing deals were the undercover shoppers offered? Ones that *sounded* great: lower interest rates, lower monthly payments, and less money down. However, when the leasing deals were analyzed by several experts, a number of overcharges were discovered: $2,100 on one lease, then $2,600 on another one, $3,000 on a third, and a whopping $7,500 on a fourth. Out of five lease deals offered to the shoppers, all five contained attempted overcharges.

At one dealer, the shopper was told that the interest rate on a loan would be 10.5%, but the salesman said he could get her a 3% rate on a lease. However, when the lease numbers were analyzed, the actual rate was 8.4%—which wasn't disclosed verbally or in the contract. The attempted overcharge: $2,100. A second dealer pulled the same stunt: told her the rate on a loan was 7.75% compared to 3% on a lease, then wrote up her lease based on 7.4% (which wasn't disclosed in the contract). The attempted overcharge: $2,600.

Two other tricks were attempted by salesmen to get more money out of the *PrimeTime* shoppers: the "secret price boost" and the "disappearing trade-in." When one of the shoppers asked about purchasing a car that was advertised for $23,999 the salesman tried to talk her into a lease, then wrote up the leasing contract based on a price that was about $3,000 higher. Of course, the higher price wasn't disclosed in the contract.

The "disappearing trade-in" was attempted by two of the salesmen visited by *PrimeTime* shoppers. At one dealer, the shopper was offered $6,000 for her trade-in, but the salesman told her that she would be better off if the trade wasn't put in writing. (He said that would lower the sales tax she paid, but no state charges tax on a trade-in.) Then the shopper agreed to put an additional $1,000 (cash) down, and the attempted overcharge got worse. Her lease payment was quoted as $364 (for 3 years) when it should have been only $153. (The trade-in and cash were not properly applied to the lease.) Total attempted overcharge: $7,500.

A second salesman also tried the "disappearing trade-in" trick on a *PrimeTime* shopper. After negotiating a lower price on a new vehicle, the shopper was promised $10,000 for her trade-in. However, the lease payment quoted for that transaction was $389 (for 3 years) when it should have been only $193. (Only $5,800 had been credited for her trade-in, not the $10,000 that was promised.) Total attempted overcharge: $7,000.

The 10 visits to dealers by *PrimeTime* shoppers resulted in 5 attempts to put them in leases containing overcharges with a grand total of $26,400. Besides the undercover incidents, *PrimeTime* also included interviews with several people who had recently leased new cars and claimed that similar things had happened to them.

Were these just isolated cases, or part of a much bigger problem? According to Florida Attorney General Bob Butterworth, it's a national problem. His office conducted a 2-year investigation of 26,000 auto leases, finding flagrant examples of fraud in about 10%. A few of the offenses: inflating price stickers used to determine lease payments, manipulating customers into leasing instead of buying, pocketing trade-in money instead of applying it to the lease, and under-valued trade-ins. Some people who signed leases thought they were buying their cars.

As a result of an investigation by Butterworth's office into Toyota's leasing practices in Florida, a settlement was announced in May of 1995. Southeast Toyota Distributors Inc. and 55 Florida Toyota dealers agreed to set up a $4.5 million fund to settle complaints regarding past leasing practices. The attorney general had accused the dealers of overcharging customers by not properly crediting down payments, rebates and trade-ins on leases.

Florida was not the only state with numerous complaints about auto leasing. Prosecutors in California and Illinois have caught a number of dealers who had been cheating people on leases, and Florida's Attorney General announced in late 1998 that car dealer investigations are now under way in at least 22 states.

When confronted with evidence of massive rip-offs by car dealers, people in the industry often try to dismiss it as "old news." They claim that dealers have cleaned up their act, that "those scams aren't being used anymore." So, is that really true?

May, 2000: Dealers Caught in Undercover Sting

On May 14, 2000 KCBS-TV announced the results of its three-month undercover investigation involving 14 new-car dealerships across Southern California. Salespeople and managers at some of the biggest dealers in America were caught by hidden cameras, lying, cheating and overcharging customers on new-car leases and purchases.

Out of 14 dealerships that were investigated, only 3 came up clean. The rest were caught using deceptive sales practices that included the following: adding expensive options to loan and lease contracts without permission or disclosure; secret price increases; secret interest rate hikes; falsely stating that there's no penalty for early termination on a lease; falsely stating that leasing was cheaper than a purchase; quoting inflated payments on loans to make lease deals look cheaper; lying about rates that customers were getting on loans and leases; falsely stating that certain options were free when their cost was hidden in the monthly payment; lying about the trade-in credit that a customer was getting in a lease; and falsely stating that leasing-to-own was cheaper than a straight purchase. One of the dealers caught in this sting was raided by state authorities two days before KCBS aired the results of its investigation. The raid was conducted by 15 DMV agents who served the dealership with a search warrant for contracts and records of their new-car transactions.

In a 1999 hidden-camera investigation by *ABC News 20/20,* car dealers in New York and New Jersey were also caught packing payments, charging for options that were represented as "no-charge" items, hiking prices without disclosure, and failing to properly credit the customer's down payment.

Automakers and dealers may claim that leasing is "the cheapest way to drive a car," but it's beginning to look like nothing more than a new way for dishonest dealers to fleece their customers.

Leasing: Concept vs. Reality

As new-car prices crept higher and higher, making them unaffordable for many people, new-car sales began to slip. The "good old days" of the auto industry saw buyers trading in their cars for new ones every 3-4 years, but car owners started holding on to them for about 7-8 years. Worse yet, since many people couldn't afford the payments on a new car, they were buying late-model, used cars instead. The automakers had to try something (besides cutting prices) to get people to buy more new cars, more often. Their solution: the savior of the new car industry, "auto leasing for the common man."

Previously used only by the wealthy and people in

17

business, auto leasing was picked up by the major auto-makers as a way to get around the affordability problem and get people into new cars. The automakers' plan was to get people into new-car leases that would expire in 2-3 years; after that, they would have to turn in their cars and start over—hopefully with more new-car leases. So the ads for "low monthly payments" were run and consumers took the bait.

When people asked how it worked, they were told, "Leasing is simple—instead of paying for the whole car, you only pay for the part you use." Rather than building equity in a car, people were told that it was cheaper to pay only the depreciation for a few years, then turn the car in and repeat the process. (That's not true if the buyer had planned to keep the car longer than the term of the lease.)

In a nutshell, leasing is *not* another way of financing the purchase of a car, because the lessee (the customer) does not own the car, the leasing company does. When the lease is up, the car still belongs to the leasing company, but the customer can't use it anymore because he has to give it back. If the car has too many miles or excess wear-and-tear, he has to give the leasing company more money to cover the damage. Should the customer wish to, he can purchase the car at the end of the lease—for a substantial amount of money, of course (usually 40-60% of the original MSRP).

In theory, auto leasing shouldn't have been a bad deal for people who buy new cars every two to three years, but something went wrong. Outright fraud is estimated in about 10% of the leases written before 1996, and a far higher percentage contain terms and costs that a smart buyer would never agree to *if* he knew what those terms and costs were—and fully understood them.

How did leasing turn out to be so bad for so many?

The answer is simple: greed and dishonesty. Since dealers were not required by law to disclose actual prices and interest rates in writing, it was fairly easy for salespeople to trick customers into leases that contained hidden charges and outright fraud.

Why Leasing Scams Work

Many people, who would normally be afraid to do anything as complicated and expensive as leasing without getting the advice of their accountant, take the advice of their neighbor (who's been overcharged on every new car he's bought) or a car salesman (who gets paid to tell buyers how wonderful leasing is).

Despite the fact that they don't understand the leasing process, many buyers fall for it because 1) even a bad leasing deal can be made to *sound* good, and 2) they're told that "everybody's doing it" (a slogan also heard around drug users and teenagers having sex). Then they trust *a car salesman* to tell them the truth and give them a good deal.

The dishonest car salesman now has an ideal situation: a customer who's convinced that leasing is "the smart thing to do," but has absolutely no idea what he is doing. Making huge profits off these buyers is easier than taking candy from a baby! Juggle the numbers, tell a few lies, and before you know it, the salesman has hit the jackpot.

What makes it so easy to pull off a leasing scam is that there are no laws requiring dealers to fully disclose all of the items and factors that are used to calculate lease payments. (Laws vary from state to state; none require full disclosure.) So dishonest salesmen are free to make up any numbers that sound good because they don't have to put all of them in writing. And without full disclosure of all items and factors in a lease—using language the customer can understand—people can't tell what kind of lease deal they're really getting.

The following sections explain the most common tricks that have been used by unscrupulous salesmen to trick their customers into bad lease deals. (If you're not already familiar with the strange language of leasing, be sure to read the section titled, "Leasing Terminology" at the end of the next chapter.)

Phony Lease vs. Buy Comparisons

Dealers have a number of tricks they can use to convince people that leasing is the "smart" thing to do. The most effective ones involve deceptions that usually go undetected, allowing the dealer to continue using them on more and more people.

Quoting "loaded" or "packed" payments has been a widespread practice in the car business, and it is very useful in tricking people into leases. The salesman simply inflates the loan payment to make it look a lot higher than the lease payment, which may also be inflated because it contains undisclosed (APR or price) overcharges. *This is why you should always figure out your own payments.*

"You'll have more equity 2-3 years later if you lease." This one fools a lot of people. Dealers fail to mention that residuals on leases are almost always inflated, which means that a vehicle's purchase option price is higher than its true wholesale value. (So there's no equity.)

A common trick that's used to make leases look better is comparing short-term lease payments with the payments on short-term loans that few people would ever choose. For example, to make a 36-month lease on a $20,000 car look even better, they could compare its $378 payment to the $488 payment on a 4-year loan. A more realistic choice would be a 5-year loan with a monthly payment of $406. (See Tables 1 & 2 in the Appendix.) Another trick that's used to make leasing look better than buying is the comparison of low payments on a factory-subsidized lease with higher loan payments on a regular purchase at the retail price. The salesman fails to mention that the lease payments are low because of a large, hidden discount in the price of the car.

On a 3-year, 8% loan, the monthly payment drops $31 for each $1,000 drop in loan amount. (See Table 2.) Any smart buyer (like you, after reading this book) could also take that big discount in a purchase, if they knew about it. Smart buyers don't pay the sticker price when purchasing, so don't let a salesman compare a discount lease with a purchase that's based on the retail price.

The "interest loss on up-front costs" is my personal favorite among phony arguments used to show why leasing is "smarter" than buying. A computer program (or chart) is used to show the customer how additional interest earned on the initial cash savings from a lease will reduce the overall cost (often by $500 to $800 or more). This argument is only valid if someone can afford the higher payments on a loan, so they would actually have extra cash to invest if they chose to lease. Since many who are leasing cars for $20,000 or less are leasing because they can't afford the higher payments on a loan, the "lost interest" argument is a phony one because many people won't have anything "left over" to invest.

COMMON LEASING TRICKS

The following tricks (and outright lies) have been widely used by dishonest car salesmen to overcharge people on leases. If you experience any of these, assume you are dealing with an unethical salesman. Then find a more honest dealership (and file a complaint against the dealer if the practices were outrageous).

There is no "interest rate" on a lease. Dishonest statement used to hide interest rate increase.

There is no "purchase price" on a lease. Dishonest reason given for not disclosing cap cost; used to hide price increase.

The cap cost number won't affect your payment. Dishonest statement used to explain higher price than one negotiated by customer.

The secret price boost. After buyer negotiates a lower price on car, salesman switches customer to a lease with a higher cap cost than negotiated price.

The disappearing trade-in. After buyer negotiates price on trade-in, full amount is not credited in the lease.

The disappearing (cash) cap reduction. Buyer is talked into putting additional cash down to reduce monthly payment, but full amount is not properly credited in the lease.

The phony low rate. Salesman quotes low interest rate on lease, then switches to higher rate. No rate disclosure on contract.

The "down payment" trick. Down payment is used to make a bad deal look good. Since down payments on leases are just monthly payments in advance (they don't build equity), always use zero-down to evaluate a lease. (Divide down payment by number of months in lease, add result to monthly payment for accurate cost.)

Deceptive advertising. Ads for low-priced cars that don't exist (or are limited to one car).

The phony "borrowing is cheaper" program. All-cash buyer is talked into leasing after being shown dishonest computer program "proving" that borrowing is cheaper than paying cash. (It isn't.) About 5,000 dealers in the U.S. purchased this program.

Inadequate disclosure. Failing to disclose any of the following in writing: cap cost (purchase price), cap reduction, interest rate, trade-in, residual, monthly payment, excess mileage charge, termination penalty, acquisition and disposition fees (if any), total due at signing.

Disadvantages of Leasing

The major disadvantages of leasing are: monthly payments that never end; higher depreciation, registration, and sales tax costs if a new car is leased every 2-3 years; higher insurance costs due to increased liability requirements and always driving a newer vehicle; and the risk of expensive charges for excess mileage, wear-and-tear, or early termination. On vehicles where the residual was increased to lower the monthly payment, the lessee may end up paying more than the vehicle is really worth if it's purchased at the end of the lease.

No matter what a salesman tells you, an honest comparison of leasing vs. buying will show that most leases not only fail to produce savings in the long run, but they often cost thousands more than a conventional purchase over a five- to six-year period.

The Cheapest Way to Drive a Car

On new cars, the biggest expense is depreciation. Since new cars lose about 50% of their value after 2-3 years, the longer you keep your car, the less it will cost to drive. *That's why leasing costs more in the long run.* However, at some point your car will start generating more expensive repair bills that might justify replacing it with a new one. For most cars, the first 6 or 7 years are usually free of major repairs, so that may be a reasonable time to keep a car before considering the purchase of a new one.

To save even more money, buy a car that's 2-3 years old and you'll avoid the biggest depreciation hit. Cars just coming off a lease are great candidates for this strategy. A 2-year-old lease car should be in excellent condition with low mileage, but its market value will be about 35-50% below original retail. Buying one of these (and keeping it at least 4-5 years) will cost a lot less over time than buying—or leasing—brand new models.

Unless you can earn a higher rate on your savings than you would pay on a car loan (legally, you probably can't), paying cash will be cheaper than financing. So, the less you borrow—and the faster you pay it back—the less it will cost you long-term.

Short-Term Leases

From 1990 to 1995, personal leasing was increasing by about 50% every year; it now represents about 35% of all new-car transactions. As more and more consumers became comfortable with the idea of leasing (without really understanding it), the automakers came up with an even better idea to increase new-car sales: the short-term lease.

For automakers, the obvious benefit of a shorter lease is that people would have to turn in their cars sooner, giving dealers more opportunities to sell (or lease) new cars. Ford Motor Co. was the first to really push short-term leasing with the introduction of its 2-year "Red Carpet" leases, and the company quickly became the industry's leader in short-term leases as a percentage of new-car sales. After seeing Ford's sales increase with this strategy, other companies began to push short-term leasing.

The "brilliant marketing strategy" of Ford may not deserve all the credit for the company's dramatic increase in short-term leases (and total sales). I recently discovered that Ford had been offering cash bonuses to its salespeople for writing Red Carpet leases. Typical bonus amounts were $75 to $100 per lease, but the bonus was increased if the new lease was a renewal. Some bonuses were as high as $500 per vehicle (and this was in addition to their normal salary and/or commission). The bonus program was started in 1989 and discontinued in April of 1995. (With incentives like that, no wonder so many Ford customers were talked into leasing.)

For consumers, there shouldn't be any financial advantages to a shorter (unsubsidized) lease, other than not having to do any maintenance beyond oil changes. Since the biggest depreciation hit happens in the first two years, and a straight lease payment is based on depreciation (and a money factor), the shorter lease *should* cost more per month than a longer one.

If a shorter lease looks cheaper, it could be a "low-mileage" lease (10-12,000 miles per year) that will cost a lot more if you exceed the mileage limit. Also, the lease might require a large down payment, or the factory could be subsidizing the lease by bumping the residual and/or reducing the money factor. Any (or all) of these tricks can be used to lower monthly payments on a lease.

The Future of Leasing

Some industry experts had predicted that the rapid growth of leasing would not continue. (In fact, some considered leasing to be nothing more than a "temporary solution to the affordability crisis" of new cars.) One of the reasons given was that more disclosure would be provided to leasing customers in the future, either voluntary or mandated by law, and the result would be a drop-off in leasing when people found out what the "details" were.

Another reason given was the flood of off-lease used cars expected to hit the market around 1997, which could depress used-car prices and cause losses for automakers who had been betting on higher residual values. After increasing an average of 8% per year from 1992-94, used-car prices had started to flatten out around 1995-96. By 1997, prices had actually dropped by about 2%.

Apparently the automakers were unaware of that old saying, "What goes up must come down." They had been inflating residuals, betting on higher used-car prices, like there was no tomorrow. Even though new-car prices had only been increasing by 2-3% per year, the automakers were counting on used-car prices continuing to rise at an unrealistic rate. (Had the increases of 1992-94 continued much longer, used cars would have ended up costing as much as new ones.)

A number of news articles have appeared since 1997 detailing Ford's losses on their off-lease vehicles. After seeing them sell at auctions for $1,700 to $6,000 less than Ford's residuals, the company started paying its dealers to keep vehicles that are turned in at the end of the lease. By reducing the number of off-lease vehicles that end up at auctions, Ford hoped to prevent further losses caused by their inflated residuals.

If used-car prices continue to drop, lenders will be

forced to increase lease payments since they're partly based on the future (wholesale) value of the leased cars. And higher payments would make leases less attractive, which could result in fewer leases being written. So automakers are now walking a tightrope of new-car prices, used-car values and leasing. Leasing became popular because many people couldn't afford to buy new cars. But new-car prices can't be cut without destroying the used-car market, which would cause huge losses for the automakers' leasing companies.

The used-car market and the growth of leasing have already flattened out (or turned downward), so what does the future hold for leasing? My prediction is that leasing will not get any more popular, it will continue to be used by dishonest dealers to overcharge their customers, and automakers will still use it to unload unpopular models.

Warning on Sub-Leasing

Many leasing customers have learned the hard way about the high costs of terminating a lease early. Unable to continue the payments, they tried to get out of their lease, only to discover that they would have to pay thousands of dollars in penalties for early termination. Desperate for a solution, they turned to a "sub-leasing" company for help in finding someone to take over their payments. In many cases, they lost even more money when the companies ripped them off by collecting money but failing to make payments on the lease.

People victimized by this practice often had their cars repossessed and their credit ruined. Because of this, auto sub-leasing is illegal in many states. It almost always violates the terms of a lease, giving the company grounds for immediate lease termination and big penalties. *Do not let anyone talk you into sub-leasing a vehicle.*

What Car Dealers Don't Want You to Know

2

When Leasing Makes Sense; What It Should Cost

Leasing is supposed to have the following advantages for consumers: less money tied up in a vehicle due to little-or-no down and lower monthly payments, no trade-in or selling inconveniences, and protection against loss due to excessive depreciation (or buying a lemon). Leasing's advantage for automakers: they get to unload a lot of new cars at big discounts—without actually cutting the "selling" prices. By offering leases with subsidized residuals or interest rates, monthly payments are reduced to entice more people to lease. And therein lies the secret to the best deals on leases, the only ones that smart consumers should even consider: factory-subsidized leases.

The perfect candidate for a lease is someone in business who needs to drive a late-model luxury car in order to project a successful image, but doesn't want to tie up lots of cash that could be put to better use. As long as the vehicle is used for business, lease payments are usually tax deductible, adding another advantage to the lower payments.

A recent ad for a 24-month lease on a Jaguar illustrated the savings from subsidized leasing on a luxury car. The Jaguar had an MSRP of $54,480 and would have cost about $1086 per month (for 48 months) with an 8% loan and $10,000 down. Using the advertised lease, the cash due at signing was only $1,398 and the monthly payment was only $699. (This lease had a price discount of over $5,000 which cut $208 off the monthly payment.) The low down payment on the lease saved $8,602 and the monthly payment was $387 less, resulting in substantial out-of-pocket savings during the term of the lease.

Of course, this lease customer would have to get another new-car lease after two years, but if they need to drive a new car anyway, this might be the most economical way to do that. Since automakers usually offer huge discounts on luxury cars through the use of subsidized leases, these are the ones that make the most sense. Subsidized leases on less-expensive models can also offer some savings, but not as dramatic as those found on most luxury vehicles.

Some dealers claim that buyers on tight budgets can also benefit from low lease payments, but those are the ones who get into financial trouble when they can't make the payments or they try to get out of the lease early. (All leases have penalties for early-termination and they can be as much as $5,000 on a $20,000 car.) For buyers who can't afford the loan payments on a new car, a wiser choice is a good, late-model, low-mileage used car with an extended warranty.

The following sections will explain how to figure monthly lease payments, and how to compare the total costs of leasing with the total costs of buying. (If you're not already familiar with the strange language of leasing, be sure to read the section titled, "Leasing Terminology" at the back of this chapter.)

How to Figure Lease Payments

There are four items that are necessary to calculate lease payments: the term (length of lease), the net cap cost (the final cap cost after any cap reduction), the residual value (estimated wholesale value at lease end), and the money factor (lease rate).

To calculate an accurate lease payment, you need to have the exact residual and money factor numbers. If you're already talking to a dealer about a specific car, ask him for those numbers, then check them out yourself to see what kind of deal he's offering. Otherwise, just use the current APR for car loans, and the residual number that's listed in the current *Automotive Lease Guide*. (See Chapter 11.)

Now we're ready to start our lease payment calculations. You can follow this by using copies of Worksheets 1 & 2 from the Appendix. We'll show how this works by structuring a 3-year lease for a typical $20,000 car, "zero down," an interest rate of 8%, and a residual of 50% or $10,000. (By "zero down," I mean no cap reduction. All leases require money at lease-signing to cover the first month's payment and the security deposit, which is equal to one payment rounded up to the nearest $25.)

The net cap cost is the purchase price of the car (minus any cap reduction), which is $20,000 in our example. And the residual value set by the leasing company in this example is $10,000 (because the car will lose 50% of its value in 3 years).

The monthly depreciation is simply [the difference between the net cap cost and the residual value] divided by the number of months in the lease. Since the lease in our example is based on depreciation of $10,000 over 36 months, we just divide $10,000 by 36 to get $277.78 for our monthly depreciation.

Figuring the lease rate is a little more work. If you don't have the actual money factor that will be used by the lender, take the quoted annual interest rate (or the typical rate charged by competing lenders, based on your own research) and divide that by 24 to get the money factor. (In our example, 8%—or 0.08—divided by 24 equals .003333) Now add the net cap cost and the residual together ($20,000 + $10,000) and multiply that number ($30,000) by the money factor (.003333). The result ($99.99) is our monthly lease rate.

All we have to do now to figure out the total monthly lease payment is to add the lease rate ($99.99) to the monthly depreciation ($277.78) for a grand total of $377.77. This figure does not include sales tax, which is based on (and added to) the monthly payment. A tax rate of 7% would increase the monthly payment by another $26.44.

So our example of a zero-down, $20,000 cap cost, 8%, 36-month lease has a monthly payment of $378. That's a straight-forward, no factory-subsidy lease. To lower the monthly payments, the residual would have to be increased (creating potential charges for excess mileage or wear-and-tear), the APR would have to be reduced, or a down payment would be required.

Comparison Example: Lease vs. Buy

If we were to buy the same car, at the same interest rate and price, the monthly payment on a 5-year (zero down) loan would be $406—only $28 more than the lease. At the end of five years, we would own a car that's worth about $6,000. Assuming that the car is sold at that point, we would subtract the $6,000 (or whatever the actual value was) from the total payments, giving us the real cost of ownership with a 5-year loan. In this example, leasing would end up costing about $4,300 more than buying over a 5-year period. (This is typical of unsubsidized leases.)

Don't fall for the sales trick of comparing monthly payments on leases and loans using the same term (for example, 3-year lease compared to 3-year loan). A lease is nothing but a long-term rental agreement, and its payment is supposed to be *a lot* lower than that of a typical loan (which would be 5 years). Why? Because the loan payment involves equity and ownership, and the lease does not.

How to Negotiate a Good Lease

If you decide to lease, make sure you don't fall for any of the tricks in this book. Do your homework on dealer's cost and incentives, then negotiate the cap cost as if you were buying instead of leasing. Find out the residual value and negotiate it as high as possible, then negotiate the interest rate as low as you can.

The residuals and APRs used by a particular lender may be fixed, but there are dozens of lenders available to most dealers, and they all use different numbers, so shop around for the best terms. Interest rates on leases are often inflated by dealers (to increase their profits), which means that it's possible to negotiate a lower rate if the quoted one was higher than a lender's base rate. Be sure to research the rates being charged by different lenders so you don't end up with an inflated APR.

Compare the dealer's residual number with the one listed in the current *Automotive Lease Guide*—if his number isn't higher, it's not a subsidized lease. Convert his money factor to an APR to see what the interest rate is. (Money factor x 24 = APR) If his APR isn't below the market rate, it's not subsidized. Remember: *If it's not a subsidized lease, it's not a bargain.*

Make sure the lease is a "closed-end" one with a maximum term of three years; any longer and you'll be paying for repairs on a car you don't own. Don't be tricked into a longer term to get lower payments. This is so important that it bears repeating: *Never agree to a lease term that's longer than 3 years.* And be sure to figure out your own payments—that's the only way to know if you're getting a good deal.

What is a good lease deal? It's one with no down payment or trade-in, 15,000 miles/year, and a monthly payment that's a lot lower than it wouid be on a 5-year loan. How much lower? *At least* enough to make up for not having any equity or car at the end of 5 years. In our example, $378 per month for 36 months—on a $20,000 car with no down—is *not* a good deal, but $300 per month would be (same term and balance).

For the best deals, pick cars with high resale values or ones that have factory-subsidized leases. And don't fall for the "down payment trick": down payments on leases are just monthly payments in advance. A 2-year lease at $350 a month with $2,000 down costs just as much as a 2-year lease at $433 per month with zero down. *Always use "zero down" to evaluate lease deals.*

If you decide to purchase the vehicle when the lease

ends, find out what it's worth (wholesale, not retail) and don't be afraid to offer the leasing company less than the residual. After all, if the residual was inflated (and most of them are), the lender will have to settle for "wholesale" if you don't buy the vehicle and it goes to auction. They might as well sell it to you at a discount to eliminate the reconditioning and storage expense of taking it back.

Leasing Terminology

Acquisition fee: Fee charged by leasing company to buy vehicle and set up lease. Also called "initiation fee." Sometimes negotiable. Typical charge: $450

Cap cost/capitalized cost: The price of the car—what the leasing company is paying the dealer. Should be negotiable. The lower this figure is, the lower your payments will be.

Cap reduction: Any down payment and/or trade-in that reduces the net cap cost (total amount financed). An increase in this figure should reduce your monthly payment and cut your financing costs.

Closed-end lease: Leasing company assumes all risk for drop in value due to excess depreciation. Customer can just walk away at end of lease. (Preferred type)

Depreciation: Difference between cap cost and residual.

Disposition fee: Fee charged at end of lease for turning in the vehicle. Negotiate this *before* signing the lease—only agree to pay an acquisition fee *or* a disposition fee, not both. Typical charge: $200-400

Early termination penalty: The price you'll pay to end your lease early. Ask what this is in advance—it could be thousands of dollars.

Excess mileage charge: Additional charge at end of lease for exceeding the mileage limit. Usually 15 cents per mile. Watch out for low-mileage leases—this charge can end up costing thousands of dollars.

Gap insurance: Policy to cover difference between balance owed on lease and normal insurance coverage. Needed in case of theft or total loss due to accident. Should be included in lease—insist on it.

Initiation fee: See "acquisition fee."

Lease rate: Monthly rate charged by leasing company, similar to interest rate. Includes both interest and profit. Lease rate = [final cap cost + residual] x money factor

Money factor: Used to determine lease rate. (This is usually negotiable—it should not be greater than the rate on loans.) Money factor = [annual interest rate ÷ 24]

MSRP: Manufacturer's Suggested Retail Price. This is almost always negotiable (except on Saturn vehicles).

Open-end lease: Lessee (customer) assumes risk for excess depreciation, might have to buy the vehicle for more than it's worth, or sell at a loss and pay the leasing company the difference. (Avoid this type)

Residual value: The estimated wholesale value of the car at the end of the lease; usually the same as the purchase option amount (this is also negotiable). A higher residual should result in lower payments, but don't buy the car at that price—offer less or walk away.

Term: Length of lease. Don't lease longer than 3 years, or you'll get stuck with expensive repair bills and excess wear-and-tear charges.

3

The Truth About "Dealer Cost"

Like any other large business, a car dealer has a number of legitimate expenses that have to be paid out of the total gross profit of the entire business. These expenses include rent (or mortgage payments), utilities, payroll, employee benefits, taxes, advertising, insurance, interest, furniture, equipment, office supplies, etc. Plus, a typical dealership represents an investment of at least $1 million (or more), and anyone who has that much money tied up in one business would expect to receive a decent return on his investment.

However, all of the revenue needed to cover those expenses does not come from car sales alone. Car dealers also have service departments, parts departments and body shops that can generate substantial revenues for the dealership.

To give one example, a dealership service department with a shop labor rate of $50 per hour and at least eight technicians (working at only 90% productivity) can easily generate $80,000 per month in gross profit from parts and labor. This figure is based on a conservative estimate of $15 per hour gross profit on parts installed by technicians, so the monthly total could increase substantially if more technicians are employed or more parts are installed.

Now add gross profits from the body shop and parts department to the $80,000 monthly gross profit from the service department, and without counting *any* profits from selling new and used cars, there seems to be considerable revenues there to help cover the expenses of the dealership.

That explanation was provided to shoot holes in a common excuse used by some dealers in trying to justify the huge gross profits they attempt to make on new and used cars. It should be obvious by now that they don't have to cover *all* their business expenses just by selling cars—and you certainly don't want to pay a large part of their overhead just because you bought *one* car from them.

For the purpose of the following discussion, we are only going to use the actual dealer's cost for one vehicle: the one you want to buy. As mentioned earlier, the dealer is free to make additional profits from other services and sales. He's even free to take advantage of other uninformed car buyers and make huge profits from their purchases; that's *their* problem, not yours. You just want the best possible deal on a new car, and you won't be able to do that without knowing how low to bid.

Many new-car buyers pay thousands of dollars more than they have to because they don't know how much profit there is in a sale at the sticker price (MSRP). If a buyer doesn't know, and he makes a low offer anyway, the salesman will say, "We couldn't possibly sell at that price. Why, that's below our cost!" The buyer falls for it, increases his offer $1,000 or more, and the seller ends up making $2,000 to $3,000 profit on the car.

Dealer Cost: The "Percent Factor" Mistake

Some car books recommend using a "percent factor" to determine dealer cost. This method involves subtracting various (mark-up) percentages from the suggested retail price, but it is not accurate enough to be of any use in to-day's rapidly changing new-car market. The factors are only rough estimates to begin with, and special packages or other promotional discounts can cause them to be off by 3-4% of MSRP (or more).

To further complicate matters, suggested list prices on options usually have a 15% profit margin, even on small-er cars that have a 6-10% margin on the base vehicle, making this method even more unreliable.

Because the percent factor is not an accurate way to determine dealer cost, I recommend using the actual "dealer invoice" figures instead.

Dealer Invoice

The "dealer invoice" figure is the amount that the dealer is billed when a new vehicle is delivered to his lot, but it is not always the true dealer's cost on a particular vehicle. The real cost may end up being lower than the invoice amount if the dealer is eligible for holdback or any of the factory-to-dealer incentives (which will be explained in the next two sections). However, the invoice figure must still be used as a starting point.

Always look up the dealer invoice figures yourself, using one of the buyer's guides or services listed in Chapter 11. *Don't ask the dealer to show you his invoice.* Why not? Because it tips him off that you don't know what you're doing. And if you don't know what the numbers are supposed to be, how will you know if you are looking at the real invoice or not? (I know this may be hard for people to believe, but some dealers have been known to make up phony invoices to show prospective buyers.)

Once you have the real invoice amount, the next step is to find out whether the dealer is eligible for any additional money from the manufacturer that will lower his cost on the car below the invoice amount. Two of these programs are "dealer holdback" and "factory-to-dealer cash incentives." Since these payments are rarely (if ever) disclosed or published by automakers or dealers, I refer to them as "secret profits."

Secret Profit #1: Dealer Holdback

Dealer holdback is a specific percentage or dollar amount that the manufacturer holds back from a dealer until a car is sold, then his account is credited for the amount withheld. The holdback allows automakers to artificially inflate the invoice price, then hold onto some of the dealer's money for a while (interest free, of course) before giving it back. And the holdback allows dealers to make an additional profit (typically $400 to $500 or more) that's not reflected in the margin above invoice.

If you've ever wondered why some dealers would be willing to show buyers the invoice, or why they would advertise certain cars for "$50 over invoice" (or even $50 below invoice), now you know. They're not giving cars away because they're just nice people (or dumb business-men), they can actually make money on those cars if there's any kind of holdback or dealer incentive. Since most people don't even know what a holdback is, or how it affects a new-car transaction, it's pure profit for the dealer. He doesn't have to negotiate with buyers over it, and he doesn't have to share it with the salesman who sells the car. (Dealers don't even want their salesmen to know about holdbacks, so many of them don't.)

General Motors, Ford and Chrysler all have dealer holdbacks that are based on 3% of the Manufacturer's Suggested Retail Price (MSRP). This gives their dealers an additional profit of $600 on cars that have an MSRP of $20,000. If those cars were sold at the invoice price (the amount that supposedly represents "dealer cost"), their dealers would still make a profit of at least $600 per car.

The following dealer holdback list was believed to be accurate at the time of publication. However, since the automakers do not want this information to become public knowledge, there may be holdbacks that are unknown outside the company, and some that are listed may have changed since publication.

DEALER HOLDBACK

Acura 2.0% of base MSRP plus another 1.5% of base
     MSRP for floorplanning allowance.
Audi No holdback.
BMW No holdback, but dealers can earn up to 2% of
     total MSRP if customer satisfaction goals are met.
Chrysler/Dodge 3% of total MSRP.
Ford/Lincoln/Mercury 3% of total MSRP.
General Motors 3% of total MSRP.
     (Buick/Cadillac/Chevrolet/Oldsmobile/Pontiac)
Honda 2% of base MSRP.

Hyundai 2% of total invoice price.

Infiniti 2% of base MSRP plus another 1% of base MSRP for floorplanning allowance.

Isuzu 3% of total MSRP plus another 1% of total MSRP for floorplanning allowance.

Jaguar 2% of base invoice price.

Kia 3% of base invoice price.

Land Rover No holdback.

Lexus 2% of base MSRP.

Mazda 2% of base MSRP.

Mercedes-Benz 3% of total invoice price.

Mitsubishi 2% of base MSRP plus another 2% of base MSRP for floorplanning allowance.

Nissan 2% of total invoice price plus another 1% of total invoice for floorplanning allowance.

Porsche 3% of base invoice price.

Saab 3% of total MSRP.

Subaru 3% of total MSRP.

Suzuki 2% of base MSRP.

Toyota 2% of base invoice price plus another 1% of base invoice price for floorplanning allowance.

Volkswagen 2% of total MSRP.

Volvo 1% of base MSRP, plus dealers can earn up to an extra $1,000 per car sold if customer satisfaction goals are met.

NOTE: For Isuzu, the holdback numbers must be added to the published dealer invoice prices. On all other makes, the holdback is already included in the invoice prices.

When in doubt, assume that a holdback of at least 2% (of MSRP) exists on the car you want and offer to pay factory invoice (or $200 to $300 over). Offer less if the dealer is getting an additional factory incentive. And remember that holdbacks are not based on volume; the amount is the same at all dealers selling the same model.

Secret Profit #2: Factory-to-Dealer Cash

Factory-to-dealer cash incentives are another way for dealers to make additional profits that would not be reflected in the spread between the dealer invoice and the sales price.

These incentives are always tied to specific models, to help increase sales of slow-moving cars that are causing inventories to rise. Like holdback money, the dealer's account is credited for the appropriate amount after the car is sold.

Factory-to-dealer incentives differ from holdbacks in two ways. They usually have an expiration date and their value may be tied to volume—the more a dealer sells of a particular model, the higher the incentive paid on all of those cars sold during the program. This is the ideal situation for the buyer because a dealer can actually make a lot more money on cars that have already been sold, just by selling one more—even if he has to sell it for a price that is far *below* dealer invoice.

Sometimes factory-to-dealer incentives are publicized in an effort to drive potential buyers into the showrooms, using ads proclaiming big savings (a "limited time offer," of course). When this is done, the customer may actually get part (or all) of the incentive.

However, the manufacturer may decide not to publicize an incentive, leaving it to the individual dealers to make their own decisions concerning publicizing or sharing the incentives with buyers. As you would expect, when given the choice, dealers often decide to keep most (or all) of the money for themselves.

When an incentive program is not made public, dealers are not required to share the money with buyers, so don't expect them to volunteer the information. They may not even tell their salesmen, because if they did, their salesmen might start accepting lower offers.

The dollar amounts of dealer incentives vary and are changed periodically, so consumers need to call a service that keeps track of current dealer invoices, rebates and incentives. (See Chapter 11.) Typical incentives range from $300 to $2,000 (or more) per car, which is additional profit for the dealer, so this information is crucial if you want to get the best deal on a new car.

Carryover Allowances

Have you ever seen those "year-end clearance sales" put on by dealers and wondered how they can make such drastic price reductions on new cars? If you thought dealers were losing money by "slashing prices thousands of dollars" just to get rid of last year's models, don't worry—they're not. Those year-end sales are always accompanied by some type of factory-to-dealer incentive to help them clear their lots, making way for the new models.

General Motors and Ford both have a regular incentive program just for year-end sales, called a "carryover allowance." When the new models come out, dealers receive a credit for 5% of the suggested list price (MSRP) on every unsold new vehicle that just became "last year's model." The carryover allowance for GM and Ford applies to all of their models (with the possible exception of some best-sellers), resulting in a substantial drop in the dealer's cost on leftover cars.

Other manufacturers who may not have a regular carryover program usually have some type of factory-to-dealer cash incentive to help get rid of unsold cars. If they failed to do this, orders for new models would be greatly reduced because dealers' lots would still have too many unsold cars.

End-of-the-year dealer incentives are usually publicized, but in some cases a manufacturer may let its dealers decide how much of the incentive to share with buyers and whether to publicize it at all. If the dealer wants to keep most (or all) of the money to himself, his salesmen may not know how much the incentive is worth. Because of this, buyers should use a service to find out what incentives are available before they start negotiating.

Customer Rebates vs. Dealer Incentives

The factory-to-dealer incentives discussed in this chapter are separate from any customer incentives, commonly called "customer rebates." Customer rebates always belong to the buyer and are not negotiable. However, car buyers are sometimes offered a choice between the rebate or below-market factory financing (see Chapter 7).

Both types of incentives—dealer and customer—may not apply to cars that are special-ordered. Customer rebate programs usually require buyers to purchase cars from a dealer's stock, and dealer incentives may expire before the car can be delivered. In this case, the dealer's actual cost on a car may be higher if it's special-ordered, and if a substantial customer rebate no longer applies, that new car could cost thousands more than one that's in stock.

National Advertising Charges

One thing to watch out for is the addition of a "national advertising charge" to either the dealer invoice or the final sales contract. If a dealer can get away with it, he may try to charge you as much as 1-2% of the sales price for advertising. These charges do not belong on the dealer invoice, *so don't pay them!*

Advertising is a normal business expense, just like

rent or employee benefits, but dealers wouldn't dare to add those expenses to the price of a new car. (WalMart doesn't tack on a charge for advertising when they sell a television set, and dealers shouldn't, either.) The only reason some dealers try this is that they usually get away with it, and when they do, it's pure profit.

Some new-car dealers have been the subjects of civil lawsuits for adding national advertising charges to their factory invoices and telling buyers that the charges were part of their invoice cost. *Don't fall for this trick.*

In many states, it is illegal for automakers to force dealers to pay into a cooperative advertising fund. And General Motors has been sued by a number of its dealers over these charges, so if dealers are challenging them, you should, too.

(You may see invoice charges described as, "regional marketing" or "local advertising associations." Unlike national advertising charges, these are usually legitimate invoice items.)

Floor Plan Charges

"Floor plan charges" are the interest costs incurred by the dealer for financing the new cars on his lot, typically at a rate of 0.6-0.8% per month based on the dealer invoice price. Some dealers try to add this onto the sales contract (just like "national advertising charges"), using it as an excuse to reject a low offer. ("Mr. Smith, we couldn't possibly sell at that price—we've paid over $700 in interest on that car.") *Don't fall for this!* Tell them you're not going to pay it.

Incidentally, dealers usually receive some type of manufacturer assistance to offset some of their floor plan costs. Depending on the price of the car, this assistance can range from $100 to $300 (or more) per vehicle. It might even be listed on the invoice as a "cost" to dealers, even though it is credited back at a later date (like hold-back). And the dealer may be getting this credit for every new car on his lot, even the ones that sell immediately (so they have little-or-no real floor plan expense). *Refuse to pay extra for this "expense."*

Interest on a business loan is just another normal business expense, one that shouldn't be added to a customer's final bill. Once again, WalMart doesn't add an interest (or "floor plan") charge to someone's bill when they buy a television set, so why should car dealers?

To respond to the excuse that interest charges on a particular car have cost a dealer hundreds of dollars: If the dealer had done a better job of marketing—including prices that are more competitive—their cars wouldn't sit on the lot so long before they're sold. So why should you have to pay extra for their poor business practices?

4

"The System"— How Dealers Make Money

Since the objective of most (if not all) dealers is to make as much money as possible, they need to have a plan. It's not enough to just advertise and sell as many cars as they can (practically everyone tries to do that, anyway), because a dealer only gets so many new cars to sell each year. Plus, he's not going to have an unlimited supply of buyers, so he needs to get as much money as possible out of every car he sells. That's where "the system" comes in, and if you don't know how it works, you'll end up paying too much for your next car or truck.

How Salesmen Are Paid

A key player in the dealer's system is, of course, the car salesman. Have you ever wondered why they'll fight so hard (and so long) just to get another $100 out of a customer? It's because, in most cases, the salesman is getting a percentage of the profit on every car he sells. (The exceptions are Saturn salespeople, who are paid a straight salary, and a small percentage of salespeople generally working in other "one-price/no-haggle" dealerships.)

Instead of a salary, most salesmen are paid a commission which is usually 25-30% of the gross profit (based on dealer invoice, not incentives) on every car they sell. This puts the size of their paychecks in direct opposition to the best interests of their customers, which could explain why the president of Land Rover once said, "You couldn't have devised a better pay plan if your intent was to screw the customer." No wonder car salesmen have such a bad reputation—they're rewarded for gouging their customers!

System Training

Extensive training programs are used on an on-going basis to make sure salesmen don't miss any opportunities to generate a profit for the dealership. Seminars, audio tapes, videos, classes, clinics and on-the-job training are all used to teach salesmen how to turn shoppers into buyers, and how to get more money out of every sale.

Entire businesses have been built around the training of car salesmen. A number of ads for sales training run continuously in trade publications, a sure sign that those companies are getting results. One ad claims that their training will increase the gross profit on each unit by $150 to $300 through F&I ("back-end") sales, promising "no fee unless you see results." Another ad promises to "build gross profit and increase F&I income."

So, whenever you're dealing with a car salesman, assume that he's a well-trained professional, even if he doesn't act like one. (That, in itself, could be an act.) Let your guard down, and you'll end up paying too much.

Their New Strategy:
Salesmen as "Trusted Advisors"

A new game plan for dealers is sweeping the country—transforming the image of the salesman from that of a "showroom shark" (I got that from CBS-TV) to that of a "professional, trusted advisor" or consultant. One goal of this new strategy is to take the emphasis off price negotiation, focusing on "value" instead. (Translation: "We don't like competition—it forces us to lower our prices. We want everyone to pay retail.")

I have two questions regarding this new plan: 1) Are the salesmen still being paid to get more money out of their customers? and 2) After everything that's happened, do you really expect people to suddenly start trusting car salesmen?

Advertising

Before a dealer can sell a car, they need a buyer, so a number of advertising strategies are used to "increase foot traffic" in a dealership. Red tag sales, Labor Day sales, Presidents' Day sales, you name it, they're all designed to bring in warm bodies so the salesmen will have potential buyers. People are led to believe that "special values are available" because there's a sale going on, but the truth of the matter is that most sales are just gimmicks. Those prices—or better—are available any day of the week to a shrewd buyer.

The only time a dealer's cost is reduced (so they can pass the savings on to you) is when the factory comes out with a special dealer incentive. Other than that, their cost is always the same, so they can sell you a car on Tuesday for the same price they quoted on Saturday. But they don't want you to know that; they want you to think that Saturday (or whatever day you're there) is the only day you can get that "low price." Their goal: getting you to buy *before* you've had a chance to shop around or think it over.

One old trick that must still work (or they wouldn't keep using it) is advertising a particular car with a real low price in large type, then explaining—at the bottom of the ad, in small print—that only one vehicle is available at that price. (Sure, that's a sleazy trick, but anything goes when you're selling cars! Besides, that type of advertising really works. And it's legal. So just ignore their deceptive tricks and remember: *They're "trusted advisors" now.*)

Where the Profits Are

New car dealers have a number of ways to make money on the sale of a new car: the "spread" between the factory invoice and the purchase price, dealer holdback, factory-to-dealer cash incentives, "back-end sales," and reselling the trade-in. To wring the maximum profit out of each customer, a dealer will try to make a profit on each and every piece of the transaction.

A dealer's attempt to profit from a high selling price on a new (or used) car may be obvious to some people, but few consumers really know how much profit is involved. And many are unaware of the additional profit a dealer makes by claiming that a trade-in is worth less— sometimes a lot less—than it really is. (If a dealer offers

more for your trade-in than it's really worth, watch out—
that's a sure sign they're making a huge profit on your
new car.) Finally, buyers who are tricked into paying for
a lot of worthless and/or overpriced services in the "F&I"
office allow the dealer to pick up another $500 to $2,000
in additional profits.

Back-End Sales: The "F&I" Office

Dealers can make a lot of profit on the "back end" of a
car sale by talking buyers into additional items or services
after they've agreed on the price of a car. These sales are
made by the finance and insurance ("F&I") manager,
who's often one of the highest paid salesmen in a dealership. If you're not prepared for his sales pitch, he can
quickly add several thousand dollars to the total cost of
your new car.

Typical high-profit, back-end items include: dealer financing, extended warranties, rustproofing/undercoating,
paint sealer, fabric protection, pinstriping, credit-life or
credit-disability insurance, and dealer prep charges.

Unless the factory is offering below-market financing
(or your credit is so bad that you can't get a car loan anywhere else), you will end up paying a lot more if you use
a dealer to finance your car. On a 5-year, $20,000 loan,
you'll pay $582 more in interest for each additional per-
centage point (and most dealers will usually try to get 2%
over the going rate, which will cost you an extra $1164
over the life of the loan). Don't fall for that old line, "It
will only cost a few more cents per month; is that worth
all the time and effort to arrange your own financing?"
Yes, it is.

Have your car loan pre-approved through your credit
union or bank before you start negotiating, and you'll
save yourself a lot of money. Credit unions usually offer

the lowest rates, but shop around before you make a decision. If nothing else, at least you'll know whether the dealer's rate is a good deal or not.

Extended warranties provide an excellent way for dealers to pick up extra profits—tell a few horror stories about expensive repairs, then offer to include the warranty in the car loan ("easy monthly payments"). How much profit does a dealer make on a warranty? Usually $300 to $500, but sometimes as much as $1,000.

You should never buy credit-life or credit-disability insurance from a car dealer; they're both grossly overpriced. If you do want either of them (and you probably don't need them), you can definitely buy them from your insurance agent for a lot less. Don't be pressured into buying these—it's against the law for a lender to require you to buy them before making a loan.

"Dealer prep" charges are a common way for dealers to pick up an easy $150 to $200 (or more) in extra profits. The factory pays the dealer for this service, so if they can charge you for it anyway, it's pure profit. *Don't fall for this.*

Rustproofing/undercoating, paint sealer, fabric protection and pinstriping are favorite high-profit, back-end items for the F&I office. They cost the dealer very little (usually 10-20% of what they'll charge you for them), and in many cases, they're unnecessary and/or totally worthless. Don't be tricked into paying for any of these.

Why pay $200 to $400 to rustproof a car that has a seven-year/100,000-mile corrosion warranty, especially when studies have shown that newer cars are far less susceptible to rust than older ones? A 1985 study of 5- and 6-year-old cars in Michigan found 20% with rust perforation. By 1989, less than 3% were found with perforations, and few of the cars inspected ever had rustproofing/undercoating done.

A number of automakers have recently come out against aftermarket rustproofing: General Motors, Saturn, Toyota, Nissan, Volkswagen, Suzuki and Subaru. Some of them warn that damage caused by aftermarket rustproofing will not be covered under warranty, and the treatment itself could void the corrosion warranty.

Regarding "fabric protection," most upholstery fabric is already treated before it's put in a car, but if you want this done anyway, just buy several cans of Scotchguard® at the store (for about $10) and do it yourself. It isn't worth the typical charge of $100 to $200.

The same goes for "paint sealer" (another $100 to $200)—in most cases this is totally unnecessary and definitely overpriced. Most new cars today already have a factory clearcoat, so any paint sealer charge is just a waste of money.

If you're tempted to buy undercoating, paint sealer, or fabric protection, call the factory's toll-free customer service number first. Ask them if those services are needed.

Car Alarms

Selling car alarms can be a very profitable sideline for dealers. The installation is usually done by outside vendors, with the dealer receiving wholesale prices and the customers paying (inflated) retail.

An inexpensive ignition/fuel cut-off system (which is not even a real alarm) typically costs the dealer less than $50 to install, but the customer's price is often $200 to $250. (This type uses a special key that's inserted under the dash to start the vehicle, but it has no real "alarm" features.)

Some dealers have installed the inexpensive systems on all the new vehicles on their lots, then if a customer doesn't want to pay for it, the dealer leaves part of the sytem in the car (with the "protection" turned off) and keeps the key—hoping the customer will change his mind and come back later to pay for it.

A "real" alarm system can usually be installed by an aftermarket car alarm company for around $200 to $250. (Look in the Yellow Pages under "Automobile Alarm/ Security Systems.") If you get one of these from a dealer, expect to pay anywhere from $300 to $600.

Final Notes

As you can see, there are many pieces to the car-buying puzzle and all of them are designed to make money for the dealer. Learn them and you won't become a victim.

In dealing with car salesmen, never forget that they are the trained professionals—and you're not. They're taught how to keep you there until you buy, and if that fails, how to get you to come back. They're taught how to turn a "no" into a "yes" and how to get a commitment to purchase out of someone who's "just looking." They're also taught how to get the maximum profit out of every sale. If you try to play their game, chances are you'll lose. (Be sure to read Chapter 12, "How to Negotiate.")

So do your homework, make an offer, then leave— with a new car, on your terms, or to make the same offer at another dealer. Dealers don't like low-profit offers, but they take them all the time. *They just don't want anyone to know.*

5

Tricks Salesmen Use

If you follow the negotiating strategies outlined in Chapter 12, you should not have to deal with a salesman to buy a new car. Unfortunately, some dealers will not allow retail customers to deal directly with their fleet or sales managers, in which case you should try another dealer. Only as a last resort should an inexperienced buyer go one-on-one with a trained, professional salesman.

Remember that almost all car salesmen are paid a commission based on profit—the more the dealership makes on a car, the more the salesman gets paid. Since a good deal for a customer is a bad deal for the salesman, a number of tricks are often used to help salesmen sell more cars for higher profits. The most common tricks used by salesmen (and their managers) are described in this chapter; make sure you understand how they work before you start negotiating.

The Question

"The question" is a tool used by car salesmen to manipulate and control buyers, for the express purpose of getting a commitment to purchase. After finding out what a customer's "hot-button" items are (for example, their desired monthly payment or trade-in value), a salesman will ask questions designed to trick the buyer into promising to purchase a car that day.

Unlike salesmen, who may not feel any moral obligation to follow through on something that's not in writing, buyers may be tricked into a deal just because they said yes to the wrong question. But remember this: You're under no legal obligation to buy a car until you've signed a contract.

The following are two very common questions used by salesmen to get a commitment: "If we can get your monthly payment down to $300 (or ??), will you buy today?" or "If I can get you $3,000 (or ??) on your trade-in, will you buy today?" When the numbers quoted are better than a buyer expected, those trick questions become very effective.

Whatever you do, don't say "yes" to any commitment questions until you're ready to buy. Instead, use vague replies such as, "I don't know," "I'll think it over," "I might consider it," or just change the subject.

If the commitment questions persist, you may be able to interrupt the salesman's strategy by asking your own trick questions. Two examples: "If I buy today, will you sell me the car at $1,000 below invoice?" or "If I buy today, will you give me $3,000 for my (worthless) trade-in?" Depending on the salesman's attitude (and how good your questions are), this ploy may amuse him or, better yet, cause him to become temporarily speechless.

Quoting Packed or Loaded Payments

Quoting "packed" or "loaded" payments is a deceptive practice that is commonly used by car dealers. When a customer asks how much the monthly payment would be on a particular vehicle, the salesman gives them an inflated figure that represents a higher loan amount or APR.

For example, if a buyer was interested in a car with a sticker (or negotiated) price of $19,000 and they had $2,000 for the down payment, the salesman might quote a loan payment of $385 instead of the correct amount, $345 ($17,000 for 5 years at 8%). If the customer agrees to that payment, they end up with a deal that costs $2,400 more than it should.

On a purchase, the inflated payment might be used to talk the buyer into a high-priced (and high-profit) extended warranty "at little-or-no extra cost." Or it could be used to put the buyer in a 12% loan when the going rate is only 8%, giving the dealer an extra $2,000 profit for the "spread" between 8% and 12%.

On a lease, the higher payment could represent an undisclosed price increase (of $2,000), or it could also be used to put the customer in a lease with a higher interest rate (once again, additional profit for the dealer).

Car salesmen frequently quote packed payments on conventional loans to trick people into leases that may contain secret price and/or APR increases. Even a bad lease deal can be made to look attractive when it's compared to a loan payment that's been inflated by $80. *And that's why you should always figure out your own payments.*

The Trade-in Buyer

If a car salesman identifies you as a "trade-in buyer," you are in big trouble. Once you say (or even hint) that you will buy a new car *if they offer you enough on your trade-in*, you are marked as a sucker who can be taken advantage of in many parts of the transaction and not even notice as long as your trade-in price is acceptable.

How this scam works is fairly simple—John Smith knows his trade-in is only worth $800 (retail), but he tells the salesman that he will buy a new car today if they will give him $2,000 for his old car. The salesman will then figure out a way to make $3,000-4,000 profit from John's new car purchase even after "giving" him $2,000 for his trade-in.

John will end up paying the sticker price (MSRP) on the new car, his interest rate will be higher, there will be a number of overpriced or worthless ("back-end") options added to the car, he'll pay $180 for "processing," $400 for "dealer prep" and "transportation," $1,500 for an extended warranty (that's only worth $500), $350 for paint sealer and fabric protection, etc.

When it's all over, and John has been thoroughly fleeced, he will tell all of his friends what a shrewd negotiator he is because the dealer paid him $2,000 for his old clunker. (Before he left, the salesman probably said to John, "Mr. Smith, don't tell anyone how much we paid for your old car—we wouldn't want everyone in town to think we're pushovers." *Yes, they would!*)

The Payment Buyer

The "payment buyer" sets himself up for a rip-off similar to that of the "trade-in buyer." After learning that the customer will buy or lease a car *as long as the monthly pay-*

ment doesn't exceed a specific figure, the salesman struc-
tures the deal to get the maximum amount of money out
of the buyer—by making sure the deal ends up at or
above the stated monthly payment. These buyers never
realize that they've been fleeced; they're just happy their
payment is "affordable."

Any (or all) of the following can be used to accom-
plish this scam: A larger down payment is required, the
length of the loan is extended to six or seven years, the
monthly payment is raised "just a little bit more," the purchase price of the car is as high as possible, the APR on
the loan is increased, numerous overpriced and/or worthless options are added, etc.

Bait and Switch

"Bait and switch" is a common trick in the auto sales industry. In this scam, the advertisement describes a great
car at a low price, but when people arrive at the dealer to
see it, they're told, "We're sorry, that car was just sold.
However, we do have another car just like it for only a
few dollars more."

A dealer is not breaking the law if their ad mentioned
(usually in microscopic print) that only one car was available at that price, but if the original car in the ad never ex-
isted, they're using an illegal business practice. If you en-
counter this, leave immediately and find another dealer.

The Deposit

In the deposit scam, a buyer is told by the salesman that
*he has to attach a deposit to his offer before the manager
will take it seriously.* The buyer's deposit is then "lost" to
prevent him from leaving after his offer is turned down,
giving the salesman more time to wear down his victim.

"I'm sorry Mr. Smith, but it looks like they've misplaced your check. I'm sure it will turn up, but while they're looking for it, why don't we try one more time to work out a deal on that car you want?"

If this happens to you, tell them to call you after the check shows up, then leave the dealership immediately. You can always stop payment on the check later if they don't give it back. Better yet, don't give them any deposit at all until *after* they've accepted your offer and you're ready to sign the final contract. Dealers negotiate without deposits all the time, so don't fall for this trick.

We Can't Find Your Keys

"We can't find your keys" is a scam that works just like the deposit trick. The salesman asks for your car keys "to have your car appraised while we're talking." The keys (and sometimes the car) are "temporarily misplaced" to prevent you from leaving so they can continue to work on you.

To avoid getting caught in this scam, always bring an extra set of keys with you when you go shopping for a car. If someone tries to pull this trick on you, tell them to call you when the keys show up, then leave the dealership immediately. Better yet, don't give anyone your keys unless you plan on going with them.

The Bump (or Raise)

The "bump" or "raise" refers to the sales practice of continually coming back to ask for more money after a buyer has made an offer. First it's $500 ("Mr. Smith, we're about $1,000 apart on this deal, but we're willing to split the difference with you. Is that OK?"), then it's $200 ("Mr. Smith, I'm working real hard to try and get this deal through for you. I think I can talk my boss into it if you can just go up another $200."), then $100, then $50, etc. As you can see, Mr. Smith was just "bumped" $850 higher than his original offer.

What's particularly outrageous about this practice is that it's probably used the most on people who are already getting a bad deal, even though the salesman claims otherwise. "Gee, Mr. Smith, you're practically stealing this car from us. Please don't tell anyone about the deal you're getting—I wouldn't want word to get out that I'm a pushover." Of course, Mr. Smith is convinced that he is getting a great deal, so he'll tell everyone he knows, which is exactly what the salesman wants him to do.

Lowballing

"Lowballing" is basically an outright lie told to a customer to get him to come in (or come back) to a dealership. This can be done on the phone, quoting someone a low price to get them to come in, then making up an excuse as to why they can't buy a car at that price. "We only had one left at that price, and we just sold it. As long as you're here, let me show you a similar car that's only a few dollars more."

This scam is also used to get a buyer to come back after turning down all of his previous offers on a car. "I'm sorry we couldn't come down far enough to reach an agreement today, Mr. Smith. We'll be able to lower the price on that car if you come back tomorrow afternoon. I'm sure we'll be able to accept your original offer."

The sole purpose of this lie is to keep Mr. Smith from buying a car somewhere else, and the lower the dishonest price, the better it works. When Mr. Smith goes back the next day, the salesman has another chance to wear him down and get more money out of him.

Turnover & The Closer

"Turnover" (or "T.O.") is what happens when a salesman realizes he's going to lose a sale (on his terms), so he "turns over" the buyer to another salesman. However, the replacement isn't just another salesman, he's "the closer." The closer may be the sales manager, or he may just be the best salesman in the dealership.

Unlike the poor buyer, who is exhausted from hours of arguing with the salesman, the closer comes in rested and with a clear head, ready to start all over again. It's just a matter of time before he wears down the buyer's resistance, who then agrees to pay far more than he intended when he entered the sales office.

Salesmen will sometimes turn over a buyer to get additional money out of him even after he's agreed to a real bad deal on a car. Once a buyer is identified as a sucker, another salesman is sent in with a different approach to milk the buyer for even more money.

The Four Square

The "four square" is an old trick, but it works quite well if the victim hasn't seen it before. Taking a sheet of paper, the salesman draws two lines, dividing the page into four squares. The salesman then asks how much the buyer would like to pay for the new car and writes his answer in one of the squares. The amount the buyer would like to receive for his trade-in goes in another square, the monthly payment the buyer would like goes in the third square, and the down payment in the fourth square. (No matter how ridiculous the buyer's numbers are, they aren't challenged at all when they are first mentioned.)

The buyer is then asked if he would buy the car right there, for the terms he specified. Of course, the buyer says he would, so the salesman has him sign the paper and put up a large deposit (the deposit scam).

The salesman then takes the buyer's offer to another room, to "get the manager's approval" (which doesn't happen). After a while he returns, telling the buyer that those numbers are not going to work. Again, the salesman uses the four-square sheet to get the buyer to commit to a reduced trade-in, an increase in the purchase price and/or a higher monthly payment.

This back-and-forth negotiation continues, with the salesman leaving the room periodically (for "approval") and the numbers constantly changing. Eventually, the four-square sheet turns into a jumbled mess and the buyer is thoroughly confused. (That's the plan—confuse the buyer, then get more money out of him.)

Assorted Lies

The following is a brief list of common lies used by dishonest car salesmen:

"That price is good for today only."
Not true—if they'll sell it today at that price, they'll sell it tomorrow at that price.

"There is no discount—our new models sell at full price."
This is only true on Saturn vehicles.

"A small discount is the best we can do."
Try another dealer—most will give substantial discounts to knowledgeable and determined car buyers.

"I'm new in this business."
If this were true, he wouldn't want you to know. It's just a

trick so you will let your guard down, thinking he's too inexperienced to pull anything over on you.

"The deal you're offering is below our cost (or we're just breaking even)—you have to pay a little more."
Assuming you're unaware of the dealer's cost, the salesman uses this trick to get more money out of you.

"Someone just called about that car you're interested in—they want to know if it's still for sale. What should I tell them?"
This is just a cheap trick to get a commitment. Sometimes it involves a phone call while you're sitting there negotiating, but the phone call is usually from another salesman or his boss, not from a legitimate customer.

6

Extended Warranties: Extra Protection or Extra Profits?

"Mr. Smith, you really should consider getting an extended warranty for your new car. Just one transmission repair could cost you $2,500 or more, but you can protect yourself against major repair bills with a great extended warranty that only costs $1,700. And we can add that into your car loan, so it will only cost you a few more dollars each month."

Sounds like a good idea, doesn't it? You can have "peace of mind" for only $1,700. But is it necessary? And is that a good price? What if the warranty costs you $2,000 to $3,000? Can you get a good warranty somewhere else for less money? The answers to all these questions can be found in this chapter.

Do You Really Need an Extended Warranty?

If you're buying a used car, it's probably a good idea—*if* you can get a good warranty at a reasonable price. On a new car, it depends on what kind of vehicle you're buying, how long you plan on keeping it, and how much the warranty costs.

What's a reasonable price for an extended warranty? For most vehicles, under $1,000 for comprehensive coverage with a deductible of $50 or less (per visit, not per item). On a used car, this should cover at least 2 years/ 24,000 miles. On a new car, this should cover at least 5 years/75,000 miles, assuming the factory warranty covers the first three years. (You'll learn where to buy warranties at discount prices later in this chapter.)

For vehicles with expensive options like four-wheel drive, turbochargers, power windows and seats, etc., it's probably a good idea to have the extra coverage. And you should definitely get a warranty if you're buying a vehicle with a poor repair history. (See Chapter 11 for sources of repair history information.)

If you're buying a vehicle without a lot of fancy options, and you've done your homework by choosing a model with a good repair history, the extra warranty may never be used. (That's what the insurance company is counting on.) Many top-rated models receive those ratings because they usually go for at least five or six years without any major repairs.

New cars today (with a few exceptions) are very reliable, and their original warranty coverage is much better than that offered in the past. Before 1992, the import manufacturers were the only ones offering widespread coverage for 3 years/36,000 miles. The Big Three automakers had only covered their cars for 1 year/12,000 miles before 1992, then they increased their warranties to 3 years/36,000 miles to compete with the imports.

With original factory warranties now covering vehicles for at least 3 years/36,000 miles—and in some cases,

4 years/50,000 miles—an extended warranty may end up providing real coverage for only a fraction of its stated term. For example, a "5/50" warranty that is purchased to cover a car with an original "3/36" is really only covering the car for 2 years or 14,000 miles. To make matters worse, if you happen to put more miles on your car than the average driver, you could easily exceed the mileage limit long before the time limit runs out.

Should a late-model vehicle require any major repairs within one or two years of the original warranty's expiration, those repairs can sometimes be done for free under a "secret warranty" or "goodwill adjustment." This is especially true when the problem is fairly common, or it is caused by an obvious factory defect. (Car manufacturers are required by law to track vehicle defects and to offer free repairs—or reimbursement—for problems that are above average in frequency.)

Although new cars today are (generally) more well-built than in the past, repair costs have increased due to greater complexity plus higher prices for parts and labor. So even though there may be less chance of a mechanical breakdown, those that do occur could be very expensive to repair. This makes the warranty issue a real gamble: If you pay a lot for one and never use it, you've wasted all that money. On the other hand, if you don't buy one and you end up paying large repair bills, you'll be sorry. So, what should you do? First, buy a good car, then buy a good warranty—but only pay about $600 to $800 for it. (Keep reading and you'll learn how.)

The Latest Warranty Gimmick:
"Money Back If You Have No Claims"

Consumers who doubt that their new vehicle will need enough repairs to justify the cost of an extended warranty have been a "tough sell" for dealers—especially when the warranty is $2,000 to $3,000. To counteract this problem, some dealers are now offering buyers what they claim is a great deal: the offer to return the full purchase price at the end of the warranty period if there are no claims.

While this might sound like a good deal, it's really just a marketing gimmick to increase sales. And it's brilliant! Think about it: You give them a large sum of money for five or six years, and if you do have any repair problems, you won't file a claim because you want your money back at the end of the warranty period. Even if you do make it to the end without a claim, and you get your money back, you've made the warranty company an interest-free loan for five or six years.

This scheme works even better if the warranty has a clause requiring claims to be made within a specified time after the repair (for example, 30 or 60 days). If a car has a 3 year/36,000 mile factory warranty, a 6 year extended warranty is only going to cover the car for 3 years or less. Let's say your car needs a $600 repair in the fourth year, but you don't file a claim because you want a full refund of the $1800 you paid for the warranty. In the fifth year, your car needs another $600 repair, but you don't file a claim. (You're still hoping to get your money back.) In year six (if your warranty hasn't expired due to mileage), another repair is needed, this time for $1,000.

What do you do now? If you file the claim, you'll only be covered for the latest repair, not the first two that cost you $1,200. You won't get your $1,800 back and your total repair costs will be $3,000 (including the warranty). If you don't file the claim, you will get the $1,800 back (without any interest), but only after you've spent $2,200 on repairs. Had you put the original $1,800 in an account paying only 5% interest, you would have had over $2,200 to pay the repair bills.

In case you're thinking that a net loss of $400 to $500 on a warranty that costs $1,800 doesn't sound that bad, let's compare it to the purchase of a 6 year/100,000 mile MBI policy for $500 with the remaining $1,300 put into an account earning 5% interest. At the end of the warranty period, you would have paid nothing for covered repairs, and your $1,300 would have grown to over $1,740. The $440 in interest almost covers the $500 cost of the warranty. Your actual net cost for warranty coverage in this example is only $60.

Those "money-back" warranties look even worse if there is a high deductible involved or if the repairs are more expensive. Worse yet, if the company goes out of business before you get your money back (this has happened to a number of independent companies), you're out of luck. One final warning: Should you sell your car or trade it in before the time is up, your warranty—and your chance of getting a refund—may be gone.

Why Dealers Push Extended Warranties

Extended warranties can add significant profits to any car sale—that's why dealers push them so hard. In 1990, the New York State Attorney General's office did a study of service contracts sold by dealers. The study found that on GM-sponsored contracts, 76% of the purchasers paid $200 (or more) over dealer cost, 16% paid $600 (or more) over cost, and 4% paid $900 (or more) over cost. The study also found that on Toyota-sponsored contracts, 92% of the purchasers paid $200 (or more) over dealer cost, 24% paid $600 (or more) over cost, and 3% paid $900 (or more) over cost. (I've seen warranties sold for $1,800 over cost.)

As if they didn't already have enough reasons to push service contracts, one company came up with a feature that dealers are sure to love. At the end of the warranty period, dealers can receive 100% of the (unused) reserves held by the insurance company and all of the investment income earned by their individual reserve accounts. (In a nutshell, if you don't use up your warranty money, the dealer gets it.)

Of course, it's up to each dealer to decide whether to share any of the money with the buyers of the contracts, so some people may not be told that their contract has this feature. Also, this type of policy could create a conflict of interest if the buyer is not told and the dealer tries to avoid performing repairs under warranty to keep more money in his reserve account.

With so much money to be made selling warranties, it's clear that buyers' best interests will often take a back seat to higher profits for dealers. Don't believe that a high-priced warranty is a good idea just because the salesman (or manager) says so.

If You Decide to Get an Extended Warranty

Should you decide to buy an extended warranty after reading about the pros and cons, be sure to do your homework first. Buy a car with a good repair history and you'll not only save money long-term, but the price of your warranty will be cheaper, too. Try not to pay more than $700 or $800 for an extra two or three years of coverage, and insist on a deductible of $25 to $50 per shop visit. Compare the coverage offered by competing plans. If you think your mileage will be above average, be sure to get a warranty with high mileage and time limits.

Thousands of people have given their hard-earned money to independent warranty companies that went out of business without paying their claims. To prevent that from happening to you, only consider policies that are backed by large, top-rated insurance companies. (Two are listed at the end of this chapter.)

Watch out for contract language stating that deductibles must be paid "per item or repair," instead of "per visit" to the repair shop, especially if the deductible is more than $25. For example, one visit to the shop where it's determined that your car needs three different repairs can cost you $300 if your policy has a $100 deductible per item (or per repair).

Another thing to watch out for is a warranty that requires you to go to a particular dealer (or shop) for any covered repairs. If you happen to be out of town, or you just don't like doing business with the shop they've chosen, the warranty may be worthless to you. Insist on a warranty that will cover repairs done by any licensed repair facility nationwide.

To convince you to pay more for a factory-sponsored warranty, some dealers may claim that credit union plans (and other less-expensive policies) will require you to pay the shop for any repairs, then file a claim for reimbursement. This is not true—most of the large companies use a corporate credit card for immediate payment of claims, so don't let someone use this scare tactic to sell you an overpriced warranty. (And don't buy a warranty without this direct-payment feature.)

Two more tips on extended warranties: 1) Don't buy one without shopping around first, and 2) Be sure to negotiate a better price if you're buying one from a dealer.

Now it's time to learn how these warranties work and where you can buy them for less (sometimes a lot less) than dealers usually charge.

Service Contracts vs.
Mechanical Breakdown Insurance (MBI Policies)

The term "extended warranty" is often used to describe the two types of coverage available to car owners: service contracts and mechanical breakdown insurance (MBI policies). Although they appear similar on the surface, there are significant differences between the two in how they are sold and how much they can cost.

Mechanical breakdown insurance is an agreement between the customer and an insurance company to cover certain repairs during a fixed time/mileage period. As an insurance product, the sale of MBIs is regulated by the Department of Insurance (for coverage and price) and can only be sold through licensed fire and casualty agents. By law, these policies must have a cancellation clause giving a buyer the right to cancel within 30 days of purchase (60 days in California) and receive a full refund. MBIs are sold by credit unions and insurance agents, and since their prices are regulated by the states, they are not negotiable.

A service contract is basically a written promise from a manufacturer (or other company) to cover specified repairs. It is not insurance, but it should be backed by a major insurance company. Since service contracts are not insurance products, there is no regulatory oversight of their prices (except in Florida), so they usually cost more than MBI policies. When a service contract is offered by the manufacturer and it merely extends the warranty past the original factory warranty period, it becomes a true "extended warranty." Service contracts are the only warranties sold by car dealers, and since dealers are free to set their own prices, they are always negotiable. Cancellation policies are usually the same as those found in MBIs.

WHERE TO BUY EXTENDED WARRANTIES AT DISCOUNT PRICES

Mechanical Breakdown Insurance (MBI Policies)

MBI policies can be purchased through credit unions and insurance agents, so they should be available nationwide. They're backed by a large insurance company, they offer direct payment to any licensed repair shop, and their coverage is basically the same as a good service contract (bumper-to-bumper, except for routine maintenance and normal wear items such as tires, brakes, wiper blades, spark plugs, etc.). MBI policies are available with deductibles of $25 or $100 (per repair visit, not per item), and their new-car policies include the following: towing up to $50 per breakdown, rental car up to $30 per day, travel interruption up to $75 per day, lost keys/lockout up to $35, and tire repair up to $15 per occurrence.

MBI policies are priced according to a vehicle's repair history; the more repairs a particular model needs, the higher the price. Their new-car ratings range from 1 to 9, with 1 representing the best cars (those needing fewer repairs) and 9 representing the worst. Cars rated 7 to 9 should probably be avoided, cars rated 5 to 6 are marginal, and those rated 1 to 4 should be safe to buy. (Cars rated 1 have such great track records that you might decide to skip the extra warranty, but that could be pretty risky on cars that are rated 2, 3 and especially 4.)

For new cars rated 1 to 4, MBI prices for 5-year/ 75,000 mile policies range from $341 to $574. For those same cars, MBI prices for 6 year/100,000 mile policies (the most popular) range from $501 to $848. (These prices are for policies with $25 deductibles; prices are lower if you choose the $100 deductible.)

MBI policies are also available on used cars that are not more than nine years old. For these policies, cars are rated from A (the best) to H (the worst). They have the same towing, rental car, travel interruption, lost keys/ lockout and tire repair benefits as the new-car policies.

For lower-mileage used cars (50,000 miles or less), two policy terms are available: 3 years/36,000 miles and 4 years/48,000 miles. For cars rated A to C, prices for these policies range from $445 to $1072. For cars with higher mileage (50,001 to 80,000 miles), MBI prices for 2 year/24,000 mile policies range from $498 to $1068 for cars rated A to C. (These prices are for policies with $25 deductibles; prices are lower for $100 deductibles.)

Other MBI policies may be available with different time/mileage combinations. The above plans were mentioned because they are the most common, and to illustrate the dramatic price differences between MBI policies and service contracts sold by dealers.

Policies regarding the sale of MBIs will vary among credit unions. While many limit sales to members of their credit union, the only requirement for membership is usually a savings account with a minimum balance of $100—a small price to pay for saving so much money on the warranty. (And they'll even pay you interest on your savings.) Some may also restrict sales to those who use the credit union for a car loan, but since credit unions often have the lowest interest rates on loans, this could result in even greater savings on a new or used car.

Any credit union can access MBI carriers, so even if your credit union doesn't usually sell these policies, they can get one for you. If you don't have access to a credit union, call the major ones in your area. Many are now interested in gaining new "members" (i.e., depositors), even if they have no professional connections.

MBI Policies: Order by Phone (38 states only)

If you can't find a credit union (or independent insurance agent) that sells MBI policies, you might be able to order one by phone. The administrator for the credit union MBI policies, Mechanical Breakdown Administrators, is able to sell MBI policies by phone or mail in most states.

Mechanical Breakdown Administrators
9419 E. San Salvador, Suite 105
Scottsdale, AZ 85261
(800) 669-0606
(480) 860-2288

At the time of publication, Mechanical Breakdown Administrators was unable to sell MBI policies in these 12 states: AL, AK, AR, HI, ME, NV, NM, NY, TX, VT, VA, WA. For current prices and state availability, be sure to call their toll-free number or visit their Web site at www.mbadirect.com.

Warranty Gold Service Contracts: Order by Phone

Warranty Gold is a major provider of service contracts, and they offer a wide selection at prices that are usually much lower than dealers. Their plans are backed by a large insurance company, they offer direct payment to any licensed repair shop, and their two best plans provide coverage that is comparable to (or better than) the coverage provided by MBI policies.

Warranty Gold offers three levels of coverage: Gold (powertrain plus), Platinum (basic "bumper-to-bumper") and Diamond ("bumper-to-bumper" plus). Their standard deductible is $50 per repair visit (not per repair/item); they also offer $0 deductible plans for an additional charge. The following plans and prices on popular models were quoted by Warranty Gold at the time of publication:

New Cars - 5 Years/75,000 Miles
Honda Accord: Diamond $779/Platinum $599/Gold $549
Chev. Malibu: Diamond $929/Platinum $654/Gold $625
Ford Taurus: Diamond $1054/Platinum $804/Gold $725
Ford Explorer: Diam. $1054/Platinum $804/Gold $725

New Cars - 7 Years/100,000 Miles
Honda Accord: Diam. $1004/Platinum $730/Gold $699
Chev. Malibu: Diam. $1129/Platinum $854/Gold $799
Ford Taurus: Diam. $1304/Platinum $1054/Gold $899
Ford Explorer: Diam. $1304/Platinum $1054/Gold $899

Warranty Gold offers other plans with different terms and coverage. (Notice that their 100,000 mile plan has one more year of coverage than the MBI policies.) They also have plans for 1993 and newer used cars with 70,000 miles or less on the odometer.

For price quotes, coverage details or any other questions, call toll-free: (877) 485-4790. You can also get free online quotes through the "CarInfo.com" Web site at www.carinfo.com (look for "$$ Saving Tips" and Extended Warranties).

Warranty Gold
901 S. Mopac, Suite 310
Austin, TX 78746
toll-free (877) 485-4790

Final Comments

If you decide to get an extended warranty for your new (or used) car, and you want the best possible deal, here's how to pull it off: Get prices on MBI policies and Warranty Gold plans *before* you finalize anything at the dealer (i.e., before you sign any contracts). Then give the dealer a chance to beat the price you got—on a plan with identical coverage.

Don't compare plans that have different terms, and don't let the dealer convince you that his plan is better when it doesn't look better on paper. If the dealer's warranty is better (i.e., same terms, but cheaper), buy it. If not, buy the MBI or Warranty Gold plan.

And finally, please do not call these companies *after* you've already purchased another extended warranty to find out if you got a bad deal. (You probably did.) If too many people do that, they might ask me to remove their names from my next book.

7

Financing:
Facts & Fallacies

Making the wrong decisions in financing a car can easily
end up costing a buyer an extra $500 to $1,000 (or more),
but most people don't even shop around for a loan before
they go to a dealer to buy a car. Instead, they trust the
salesman to give them advice (and a good deal) on the financing phase of their transaction. And that's exactly the
way car dealers want it, because a large part of their profit from car sales is generated in the finance and insurance
office.

    A smart buyer does his homework first, making sure
that the interest rate he ends up with is the best that's

available. He knows exactly what he wants and how much it's worth, and when he leaves the "F & I" office, he hasn't bought anything that he didn't want before he went in there.

Finding the Best Rates

Interest rates on car loans can vary significantly from one lender to another, so be sure to check the rates available at a number of banks and credit unions. Banks usually have reduced rates on loans for customers who set up an automatic-payment plan, and credit unions often have rates that are lower than many banks. Most credit unions also have mechanical breakdown insurance (extended warranties) at prices that are hard to beat, so if you don't belong to one, it might be worth joining. (See Chapter 6.) Be sure to have an outside loan pre-approved before you go to a dealer to negotiate on a car.

When 8% Financing Is Better Than 3%

Whenever you see low-interest factory financing, it's almost always offered instead of a customer rebate or dealer incentive that results in a price decrease. Rates as low as 5.9%—or even 2.9%—may sound like a bargain, but in some cases it might be smarter to take the rebate and go with a higher interest rate. As the following chart shows, a lower rate will be worth more on a longer-term loan, and also on a loan with a larger balance.

> each 1% reduction in interest rate saves:
> 3-yr. loan: $16.56 per $1,000 borrowed
> 4-yr. loan: $22.08 per $1,000 borrowed
> 5-yr. loan: $28.80 per $1,000 borrowed
> 6-yr. loan: $34.56 per $1,000 borrowed

Here's how to figure out which is smarter: Let's say we're offered a $1,500 rebate or 5% financing on a 4-year loan, and we need to borrow $15,000. The going rate on loans right now is 8% and we need to figure out whether to take the low-rate loan or the rebate. Using the number from the chart, first multiply the 4-year savings ($22.08) times the number of thousands borrowed (15), which gives us $331.20. That's the savings for a 1% reduction, but we were offered a 3% reduction, so we multiply that final number ($331.20) by 3 to get $993.60. So the 3% rate reduction is worth $993.60 on a $15,000 loan for 48 months. In this case, the rebate would be a better deal than the low-rate loan, so we would take the $1,500 and get an 8% loan, coming out ahead by $506.40.

"Upside-Down" Car Owners

"Upside-down" is insider language for owing more on a car than it's worth. The most common ways for this to happen are: 1) paying too high a price for a particular car, 2) not having a big enough down payment, 3) the term of the loan is too long, and 4) the interest rate is too high. Unfortunately, most people don't even know they have this problem until they try to sell their car early in the loan, then they have to come up with additional cash (over and above the purchase price) just to sell it.

Trading in an "upside-down" car on another one just makes the problem worse, because the salesman will have to make sure there's a huge profit margin on the new(er) car to cover the loss on the trade-in. Now the buyer has been victimized again by paying too much on another car.

The only solution to this problem—other than coming up with extra cash to sell the car—is to keep it until the loan has been paid down far enough to bail out.

No Pain, No Gain:
The Sober Way to Finance a Car

I'm not going to beat around the bush—the intelligent way to finance a car is to make a down payment that's as big as possible, and then make large monthly payments. The less you borrow, and the faster you pay it back, the less your overall finance costs will be. An added bonus to following this advice is that you probably won't find yourself in the "upside-down" condition mentioned earlier. *Just remember: no pain, no gain.*

I know a lot of people won't like this advice, but I named this section "The Sober Way to Finance a Car," not "The Painless Way..." By taking the "sober" route to financing, you avoid the "hangover" of watching thousands of your hard-earned dollars go down the drain. The following chart shows how much interest can add up in different term loans:

$20,000 loan @ 9% (numbers rounded off)			
	3 yrs.	4 yrs.	5 yrs.	6 yrs.
mo. pay.	$636	$498	$415	$361
total cost	$22,896	$23,894	$24,912	$25,963
total interest	$2,896	$3,894	$4,912	$5,963

$16,000 loan @ 9% (numbers rounded off)			
	3 yrs.	4 yrs.	5 yrs.	6 yrs.
mo. pay.	$509	$398	$332	$288
total cost	$18,317	$19,116	$19,930	$20,771
total interest	$2,317	$3,116	$3,930	$4,771

As you can see, a bigger down payment and/or shorter term can save thousands in interest over the life of the loan. For example, on a $20,000 loan, choosing a 5-year term instead of a 6-year one saves $1,051 in interest, but the monthly payment is only $54 more. *A little pain, big gain.* Pocket the savings and apply them to the down payment for your next new car—after you've kept the first one for at least 6 years to get the maximum benefit out of owning.

With a bigger down payment on your next new car, you should be able to get a 4-year loan—with payments close to those of a bigger loan for 6 years. Now you'll save $1,655 in interest just from the difference between 4-year and 6-year loans with $4,000 down. Compared to the 6-year $20,000 loan, switching to a 4-year loan with $4,000 down (on the next new car) will save $2,847 in interest. *A little pain, big gain.*

The opposite of what we just outlined is a recipe for financial disaster: pay more than a car is worth, put nothing down and finance the balance for at least 6 years. By the time your loan is paid off, you will have wasted at least $3,000 to $4,000 and you'll probably be unable to come up with any money for a down payment on another car, so a salesman will put you into another 6-year loan (or talk you into leasing). You will then make payments for the rest of your life.

How to Calculate Loan Payments

The following chart can be used to figure out loan payments for varying amounts and interest rates. For example, to figure out the payment on a $15,000 loan at 9% for 5 years, just multiply the number from the chart ($20.76) times the number of thousands borrowed (15) and you get a monthly payment of $311.40. *Remember: borrow as lit-*

tle as possible and pay it off as fast as possible.

| Rate | Monthly Payment per $1,000 Loan | | | |
	3 yrs.	4 yrs.	5 yrs.	6 yrs.
8%	$31.34	$24.41	$20.28	$17.53
9%	$31.80	$24.89	$20.76	$18.03
10%	$32.27	$25.36	$21.25	$18.53
11%	$32.74	$25.85	$21.74	$19.04
12%	$33.22	$26.34	$22.25	$19.55
13%	$33.70	$26.83	$22.75	$20.07

Financing Your Extended Warranty

A common mistake buyers make is deciding to get an overpriced extended warranty (or service contract) from a dealer because they can include it in the car loan, allowing it to be paid off with "easy monthly payments."

For example, a $1,200 service contract in a 5-year loan at 10% will cost $25.50 per month, with a total cost of $1,530. If we bought the same factory-sponsored service contract somewhere else at a discount (see Chapter 6), we would only have to pay $700, and even if we had to put that on a credit card at 18% for three years, that would only cost $25.31 per month—for three years, not five. Total cost: $911 if we take 3 years to pay it off. By paying an extra $10 every month, we could pay it off in two years. Total cost that way: $839—a savings of $691 over the service contract in the car loan.

One more tip: If we were to pay cash for an "MBI" warranty, we would only pay about $500 to $600. The savings: over $1,000 compared to a warranty that's added to a car loan. As you can see, a different approach to the extended warranty game can result in dramatic savings.

Other "F&I" Deals to Avoid

Be prepared for a number of sales pitches from the finance and insurance salesman, because a dealer might make more money putting additional "stuff" on your contract than they make on the car itself. Rustproofing or undercoating, paint sealer, fabric protection, credit life or disability insurance, car alarms and extended warranties are all big money-makers for dealers.

A car alarm that costs $500 to $600 at the dealer can often be purchased somewhere else for $150 to $200, and extended warranties can be purchased elsewhere (or negotiated) for a much lower price. The rest of the items mentioned above are simply overpriced and/or worthless, so refuse to buy any of them.

The "Financing Is Cheaper Than Cash" Lie

Beware of phony charts or computer programs that are used by dishonest salesmen to convince buyers that financing is cheaper than paying cash. *It isn't.* They just want to convince you to finance so they'll have another opportunity to make money.

For most people, paying cash will always end up costing less than financing, even when below-market factory financing is offered at rates that look too good to be true. That's because buyers who use the special financing are usually giving up a rebate or discount in the price, so after you factor in the higher price with the total interest paid over the life of the loan, it adds up to a lot more than someone would have earned from investing the total amount.

In addition, any investment earnings will be reduced by income taxes—at least 28% for most people—making the cash deal look even better. Since the "real" (unsubsidized) cost of financing is usually around 8-10%, you would have to make 12-15% on your investment to come out ahead of the cash deal (after taxes). Unless you're a loan shark, you're probably not going to make anywhere near that much, so the "financing is better" argument is a dishonest one.

Comparing Leasing With Buying

When comparing leasing with buying, be sure to include all leasing fees paid up front, any down payment or trade-in, the total of all monthly payments (including tax), the residual and any disposition fee. That's the total cost of a lease. The cost of buying is the total of all monthly payments, plus any down payment, fees, or taxes paid up front. (You can use the worksheets in the Appendix.)

Beware of any comparison showing an advantage to leasing over buying—there usually isn't any. If a leasing sales pitch sounds too good, it probably involves some deception. (Be sure to read Chapters 1 and 5.)

Using Home Equity Loans for Cars

Ever since Congress ended the interest deduction for all installment loans except mortgages, some "financial experts" have been recommending that people use home equity loans to buy cars—just for the tax deduction. While the deduction *might* lower the cost of a car loan, I'm not very comfortable with the thought of mortgaging the house to buy a car. Should something happen, instead of just having the car repossessed, a person could lose their house in a foreclosure.

Besides the little foreclosure issue, there may not be much of an advantage to using a home equity loan to buy a car. Since equity loans are real estate loans, they often involve set-up costs that can total several hundred dollars (or more), wiping out any possible savings from the interest deduction. And the interest rate on equity loans is usually a little higher than car loans, making them even harder to justify.

My biggest objection to using home equity loans for buying cars is the strong possibility that many people would just get into trouble using them. After all, most people leasing cars today are only doing that because they can't afford the down payment and monthly payments on a loan. Without the shorter term of a car loan, many people would take a lot longer to pay off their car, driving up the total interest cost on the loan and possibly taking ten years or more to pay it off. Their loan could last longer than the car!

What Car Dealers Don't Want You to Know

8

Your Old Car: Trade-in Tips

The best advice anyone can give on how to get the most
money for your trade-in is: *Don't do it!* Car dealers "buy
low and sell high"—that's how they make money—so
don't be fooled into thinking that a dealer is going to pay
you "fair market value" for your old car.

Any offer from a dealer that is significantly higher
than the wholesale value of your old car is a good indica-
tion that you are paying too much for the new one. In this
case, the dealer will just use part of the huge profit he's
making on your new car to knowingly "pay" more than
the trade-in is really worth. Never forget that you are

dealing with a professional and if anyone is going to be taken advantage of, it will be you, not the dealer.

The following dealer ad is a classic example of how buyers are fooled into thinking they are getting a great deal: "We'll give you one thousand dollars, or more, for your trade-in when you buy a new car or truck. That's right, guaranteed! One thousand dollars, or more, for any trade-in, running or not. So drive it, push it, or tow it here today take advantage of this special offer!" This dealer is just going to make sure his profit on the new car is high enough to cover a worthless trade-in.

To get the best possible price for your old car, you must sell it yourself. I know this is an inconvenient and sometimes unpleasant experience, but the more your car is worth, the more money is at stake. A typical five-year-old, mid-size domestic car has a difference of (at least) $1,200 between low and high retail values, and dealers are only going to pay wholesale (which is usually *at least* $900 less than low retail) on trade-ins.

As you can see, this can quickly add up to thousands of your hard-earned dollars going into the dealer's pocket. With this much money at stake, isn't the inconvenience worth the $1,200 (or more) you'll save? Even if it takes ten hours to prepare, show, and sell your old car for $1,200 more than a dealer would give you on a trade-in, that works out to $120 per hour—tax free! Few people make anywhere near that kind of money at their job, but they "don't want to be bothered" by selling their own car. Amazing!

Since the best deal for you is to sell your old car yourself, the following sections are included to provide some tips that will help you get the highest price for your old car. For those who insist on trading in their old car, in spite of the fact that they will end up with less money, a section is included at the end on trade-ins.

Research

Whether you are selling your old car or trading it in, you need to do some research if you want to get top dollar. First, determine the approximate fair market value of your car. Start with the information provided in several paperback guides for used car prices (for example, *Kelley Blue Book Consumer Edition* or *Edmund's Used Car Prices*). These can be purchased at most bookstores for about $10, or if you're lucky, your local library might have them.

Be sure to check at least two different guide books, because the prices given are not always the same. For example, *Edmund's Used Car Prices* lists current wholesale (what a dealer would pay) and average retail, but no price ranges. The *Kelley Blue Book Consumer Edition* provides figures for two categories: "retail/good condition" and "retail/excellent condition," but no wholesale price figures for trade-ins.

For the purpose of determining the market value of a car, "good condition" means that a vehicle has no major defects or mechanical problems. The interior, body and paint have only minor blemishes, and the tires have substantial tread remaining. Some reconditioning and/or minor repairs are needed.

"Excellent condition" means that a vehicle is free of visual and mechanical defects—it looks and runs great. The interior, body and paint have no visible defects, and the tires are new (or like new). No reconditioning or repairs are needed.

After you have determined the "book" price range for your car, consult your local newspaper classifieds to see if there are any similar cars for sale in your area. Compare their condition, mileage and equipment with yours, then take into account their book value and how long they've been on the market (to determine whether they're overpriced).

Actual selling prices of similar cars in your area will determine the true market value of your car, to a greater extent than the price guides, but it's still a good idea to look up the numbers, anyway. Knowing the approximate value of your car could save you from "giving it away" by pricing it too low. Don't try to compete with other cars that are advertised at "distress sale" prices, or are priced low because they're "lemons."

Preparing Your Car

Once you have figured out the price range for your car, have it inspected for safety and mechanical defects, then get estimates for any problems that were found. If your car received a clean bill of health, get it in writing to show prospective buyers. Written inspections from an impartial source can help you get top dollar for your car, especially if done by AAA. Inspections done by repair shops may or may not be taken at face value, depending on the buyer.

If a number of items need repair, determine which ones can be fixed without spending a lot of money. Expensive repairs done before selling a car rarely increase its value more than a nominal amount, because the "book value" assumes that a car is already in good condition. That's why it's a good idea to first determine your car's fair market value—so you don't spend $1,500 repairing a car that will still only be worth $1,800 when you're done.

Repairs that are safety-related or ones that will improve the driveability of your car are usually worth doing before putting it up for sale, especially if they can be done at a reasonable cost. After road-testing a car with bad steering or brakes, or one that runs poorly, a smart buyer will wonder why those problems weren't fixed and may assume the car needs expensive repairs. This will result in lower offers on your car—or worse yet, no offers at all.

Make sure all accessories, lights and equipment are working properly. Check all of the tires, including the spare. If any of the tires need replacing, shop around for the lowest price on new radials, then replace them in pairs only (both fronts or both rears). A car with matching tires will look and drive better than one with three or four different brands.

Change the oil and filter, then check the coolant (antifreeze) in the radiator—if it doesn't look clean, flush the radiator and put in new coolant. Smart buyers will take a look at the oil and coolant to see if the car has been properly maintained, so make sure those fluids look new. If the air filter is easy to remove, make sure it's clean, too.

In determining which items to fix before selling a car, keep this in mind: the most cost-effective repairs are the ones that make the most noticeable improvement for the least amount of money, so don't spend a fortune—you won't get it all back.

When you're ready to put the car up for sale, get a smog inspection and certificate so you can show potential buyers that your car is in good shape and it's smog-legal. As the seller, you are legally responsible for delivering a vehicle that (1) has all the required smog equipment, in working order, and (2) will pass inspection.

You can't avoid liability by selling the vehicle "as is" and telling the buyer that the smog equipment is their problem. I've seen vehicle sales unravel after-the-fact when the buyers took the sellers to court over expensive smog repairs. A seller could end up having to pay a buyer a large amount of money (as much as the sale price), or taking the car back (even if it's in worse condition), so make sure your car passes inspection *before* putting it up for sale.

Have the car detailed (or do it yourself) so the body and paint look as good as possible. Make it shine! The interior should look and smell clean. Clean out the trunk. Remember this: The fewer things a buyer finds wrong, the better your chances of selling for a good price. (That means replacing the "coat-hanger" antenna with a real one.)

One final note: Detail the car *after* all repairs, reconditioning, smog inspections, etc., so it looks great when potential buyers show up.

Advertising Your Car

The traditional (and unimaginative) way to advertise your car is an ad in your local newspaper. This is also a very expensive way to advertise, with results that vary greatly from one seller to the next.

If you're a woman who lives alone, it may not be wise to let strangers know where you live, let alone inviting them to your house. For women using this method of advertising, it might be a good idea to have a male friend show the car (at his house). Or pick a public place to meet and bring a friend with you. This is especially important when it comes to a stranger road-testing your car. Some women have been assaulted in the past by men using the classifieds to find potential victims. Don't take chances— take a friend with you, instead.

If a stranger takes your car for a spin by himself, he might damage it (or steal it). And don't assume that the car he left at your place belongs to him; it could be one he "borrowed" from another seller. Women who insist on staying with the car should bring a friend along.

Some people recommend letting potential buyers go

on road-tests by themselves, reasoning that your personal safety is more important than the money you would lose if someone damaged or stole your car. This *is* a good point, but using the "buddy system" is a lot safer than going by yourself.

Newspapers are not the only way to advertise your car. Other methods include general-purpose direct-mail advertisements (like the *Pennysaver*) and specialized ones (like *Auto Trader*) that can be found on racks at grocery and convenience stores. These are usually less expensive than advertising in major newspapers, but results vary.

Instead of print advertising, some sellers choose to display their car—with a "for sale" sign—where it will be seen by many. This can be done (for a fee, of course) on a number of car lots that display "private party" cars for sale. Not to be confused with "consignment" lots where the vehicle owner is guaranteed a set amount and the lot keeps all the money in excess of that figure, a private party car lot is simply a "physical classified ad" where potential buyers can see many cars for sale by private parties, all on one lot.

Depending on where you live or work, you may be able to display your car (for free, of course) on a vacant lot or parking lot next to a busy street. All you need is a "for sale" sign listing the price, contact phone number, and any other vital information that will fit. I used this method to sell a car for $900 more than the dealer offered as a trade-in, and it sold—for the price I was asking—the first day it was displayed.

In some areas, there may be laws against displaying your car on public streets. Also, some vacant lots and parking lots may have signs prohibiting this practice, with threats of towing away cars that ignore the warning signs, so be sure to check before trying this.

If you can't find a good location to do this for free, you might try offering to pay a service station or other business owner to let you display your car on his lot, in full view of a busy street. Even if you end up paying $10-20 to use his lot for a weekend, that's still cheaper than advertising in the newspaper. When you're negotiating, remind the lot owner that any amount is more than that space has been earning so far.

Negotiating With Buyers

How you price your car, and how you negotiate, should depend on how long you are willing to have a car for sale. The process is inconvenient and frustrating for many, so if you would like to get it over with as quickly as possible, then price your car a little lower than the competition and accept the first reasonable offer. On the other hand, if you love selling things, you may want to hold out for top dollar, but this will require greater sales ability and more advertising expenses because it will take longer to sell your car.

Knowing your competition can be a big help in countering objections and lower offers. Check out similar cars for sale in your area to see how yours measures up, then use this information to convince potential buyers that your car is a better deal (for example, "my car has newer tires, a rebuilt engine, lower mileage," etc.). Any documentation or warranties you can provide for major items is a plus, as is a written record proving that the car was properly maintained.

If you would like to learn the art of selling or negotiating, visit your local bookstore or public library and study those subjects. There have been a number of books published recently by some of the greatest salesmen and negotiators in the business.

When You've Got a Buyer

Whatever you do, don't take a personal check as pay-ment-in-full on a car, unless you cash the check at the buyer's bank *before* giving him title and possession of the car. If a buyer insists on a same-day transaction, make him pay in cash or a verified cashier's check.

To avoid receiving parking tickets and other traffic vi-olations that should be going to the new owner, make sure the title transfer is recorded immediately. Don't as-sume that the buyer is going to do this, because even if you send in the notice that you have sold your car, if the buyer fails to complete the title transfer, you could still end up in court trying to convince a judge that those tick-ets belong to someone else. Worse yet, if the buyer gets in an accident, you could be sued.

The easiest way to make sure the title transfer is re-corded is to have the buyer meet you at the motor vehicle department. You bring the car, along with a completed bill of sale, the title and registration, and a current smog inspection certificate. The buyer brings the money. Give him possession of the car *after* you have the money in your hand and the necessary paperwork has been signed and turned in.

One last tip: Make sure you have included the words "this vehicle sold as is" on the bill of sale. Otherwise, if something goes wrong with the car after the sale, the buy-er may claim that you gave him some kind of verbal promise that the car was in perfect condition.

Dealer Trade-in

If you still insist on trading in your old car (in spite of the fact that you will end up with less money), get bids from several dealers before agreeing on a price. Locate the used-car manager and ask if he's interested in buying your car. If he is, have him make an offer—preferably in writing. Do this at several dealers (and maybe some used car lots, too) and you will quickly learn the wholesale value of your car.

See how the dealers' bids compare to the values listed in *Edmunds Used Car Prices* or the NADA price books, then try to negotiate a better price with the highest bidders. This will be easier to do if your car is in excellent condition, because they know it will bring top dollar on their lot.

Higher bids from competitors can sometimes be used to persuade your dealer (the one who's selling you a new car) to raise his offer. However, if you've done a good job of negotiating away most of his profit on the new car, he may not be able to go much higher on your trade-in. In that case, you'll soon learn the depressing truth about how much you are really getting for your old car.

9

One-Price & "No-Haggle" Dealers

If car dealers could create a "dream world," it would no doubt feature an endless stream of customers who were not only willing, but happy to pay the sticker price on new cars—without any haggling. Of course, to make this work, every dealer in "dream world" would charge the same price for a particular model, eliminating (evil) competition that only forces businesses to lower their prices. To make the dream complete, all of the sticker prices would be high enough to guarantee that every dealer would make more profit on every sale than they could make in a competitive environment.

Sound like a silly fantasy? Not at all! "Dream world" has been a reality for Saturn dealers since the 1991 models came out although the company hasn't been much of a money-maker, it has succeeded in making everyone pay retail for its cars. Other dealers have changed from skeptics to envious competitors, and some of them have even tried to copy the "Saturn experience."

You've probably seen manufacturers and dealers advertising one-price or "no-haggle" deals on new cars. If you're the type of person who hates the negotiating process, a "no-haggle" deal may sound attractive, but are their prices really non-negotiable? The following sections explain the differences between "the real thing" and the copycats, and how you can take advantage of those differences to get a better deal.

Saturn: The Only True "No-Haggle" Dealer

At the present time, Saturn dealers have the only true non-negotiable prices in the country. Every Saturn buyer pays retail (MSRP), even if he's a "shrewd negotiator," and customers seem to love it—almost as much as the dealers. How did Saturn manage to pull that off? By giving exclusive territories to a small number of dealers, so they wouldn't have to compete with each other by lowering prices. Also, having a limited supply of cars helped to keep demand—and prices—high.

Saturn sales associates are trained to help customers fall in love with the car, and since there's nothing to discuss regarding price, they can focus all their talents on convincing people that the Saturn is the best small car on the market. Prospective buyers are encouraged to step on sample door panels to demonstrate their resistance to scratches and dents. (This *is* an impressive demonstration.) Design, construction and safety features are all emphasized in a professional presentation.

The only thing missing at a Saturn dealer is sales pressure. Their sales people are paid a salary instead of commission, eliminating the pressure to "close the deal and soak the customer for as much as you can." This is all part of the "Saturn experience," designed to be the most enjoyable car-buying visit anyone has ever had.

As enjoyable as this is for buyers, it's far more enjoyable for dealers—they get retail for every Saturn they sell, and the profit per car is much higher than it would be in a competitive environment. All 1995 Saturn base prices (and options) had a 13% profit margin, about twice the average profit on a similar car with a negotiable price. The following dealer cost vs. retail price information illustrates the larger profit margins on several '95 Saturn (base) models compared to several '95 Ford Escorts.

	Retail	Invoice
Saturn SL 4-Dr, 5-speed	$9,995	$8,696
Saturn SC2 2-Dr, auto.	$13,815	$12,019
Escort 3-Dr, hatchback	$9,580	$8,867
Escort GT 3-Dr, hatchback	$12,720	$11,726

As you can see, the lowest-priced Saturn model with no options or add-ons still made a $1299 profit for the dealer, compared to a $713 profit on the lowest-priced Escort. (These profit figures do not include the 3% dealer holdback, which adds another $300 or $400 to the profit margins.) Higher-priced Saturn models, especially those with options, can generate profits exceeding $2,000 per car. No wonder Saturn dealers love their little monopoly, I mean arrangement!

The above figures also illustrate one of the major accomplishments of Saturn: getting people to (happily) pay more for cars with fixed prices than they would have to pay for similar cars with negotiable prices. Ford Escorts are similar to Saturns in size, quality and features, but Saturns cost $500 to $1,000 more based on the retail prices. And since Escort prices are negotiable, no one has to pay retail, making the difference even greater.

So far, the success of the "Saturn experience" seems to be more the result of clever marketing and a "unique showroom atmosphere" than having a superior car. According to the frequency-of-repair records compiled by Consumer Reports, 1991 and '92 Saturns had a lot more repair problems than the later models, but that didn't seem to have much effect on customer satisfaction. Saturn owners loved the cars and "the experience" anyway.

I guess the secret to Saturn's high customer satisfaction ratings during the first two years was the illogical attitude, "I don't care if I pay more, as long as no one else pays less than I did." This attitude continues today, with many people willing to pay a premium for the enjoyable "Saturn experience." (Maybe what these consumers are really saying is that they're willing to pay an extra $500 to $1,000 just to avoid dealing with a high-pressure salesman.)

The Copycats:
One-Price & Value-Pricing Dealers

Saturn's success did not go unnoticed by other manufacturers and dealers, who were green with envy over the high Customer Satisfaction Index (CSI) ratings recent buyers had given the Saturn dealers. And all of those people paid the sticker price! After suffering for years from low CSI numbers and shrinking profit margins (due to competition), some companies and dealers are now trying to duplicate the "Saturn experience."

General Motors' "Value Pricing" programs were designed to offer substantial discounts on a number of specially-equipped models, at supposedly non-negotiable prices. To make the change to "one-price" sales, the sticker prices were lowered far below the usual MSRP. (GM didn't lower the dealers' cost though, they just reduced the margin over invoice.)

To make the change complete, a new sales atmosphere had to be created by retraining the sales staff to treat customers in a professional, no-pressure manner. In the past, many potential car buyers felt that negotiating with a dealer was about as enjoyable as having a root canal, so dealers have set up extensive training programs to eliminate the high-pressured, commission-sales atmosphere. Salesmen at some dealers are now paid a higher salary instead of straight commission.

GM's Value Pricing dealers have been trying to convince customers that their prices are not negotiable at all, but they haven't been totally successful. Without much effort, many buyers have talked sales people into lowering prices by several hundred dollars. Others have used a car buying service to get substantial discounts off the suggested "non-negotiable" prices.

For example, a car that used to retail for a negotiable $20,000 might now be "value-priced" at $19,000—which is still about $1,200 over dealer invoice. The dealer also gets a 3% dealer holdback, adding another $570 in profit to the $1,200. The total profit of $1,770 allows room for some price-cutting to close the sale, and that's exactly what happens at most of these dealers—they cut prices.

The newest arrival on the "one-price/no-haggle" scene is the Oldsmobile division of General Motors. Its market share had been sinking lower and lower, and rumors had begun to spread throughout the industry that the division was going to be eliminated. GM repeatedly said that it remained committed to the Oldsmobile line, but the rumors persisted. Average sales per Olds dealer dropped to 100-150 cars per year, compared to 400-800 for a number of other dealers, and the division needed to make some drastic changes. (Maybe they should have tried changing the name to "Youngmobiles" to make them sound more attractive.)

Oldsmobile General Manager John Rock decided that the cure for slumping sales was to pattern the division after Saturn. The goal was to have a one-price/no-haggle, pleasant car-buying environment—where every buyer would (gladly) pay retail.

However, Rock's plan had two big holes in it: First, Saturn can get away with their no-haggle prices because there are so few Saturn dealers that they have a virtual monopoly, but there are too many Oldsmobile dealers in the country to stop them from cutting prices to compete for sales. Second, the Olds dealers seem to be divided on their support for the new program—some liked it, and some complained loudly by writing open letters in trade publications.

For example, one Olds dealer who supported the new program said they were making over $1,600 gross profit per car, while another dealer complained that their new-car profit had dropped $200 per unit. (If those two dealers were *averaging* $1,600 to $1,800 profit per car under the old "start at sticker and dicker" plan, they either had a lot of unsophisticated buyers who overpaid, or they made $3,000 to $4,000 per car from a few "pigeons" to make up for the rest.)

Some Olds dealers said they were behind the "no-haggle" program, but they needed more margin to use with customers who still wanted to negotiate! They also said they could use more margin for customers who are "upside-down" (owing more on their car than it's worth) or need more for their trade-in. Apparently, not everyone is embracing the new program.

Other manufacturers have offered "one-price" deals to increase sales on certain slow-moving models, but these weren't really non-negotiable prices. For example, some Ford Escorts and Thunderbirds were supposed to have "reduced, no-haggle prices," but many dealers cut prices even lower to sell more cars.

Making the transition to "one-price" from "start at sticker and dicker" is proving to be a tough sell after decades of doing business the old way. When customers are told how the new "professional, dignified, one-price program" works, many buyers have expressed disbelief— "Sure, I understand how it works. Now, let's talk discount!"

Buyers may be wise to not believe statements that everyone will pay the same price for a particular car. A 1992 study of two dozen dealers who switched to "one-price" selling revealed that one-third of them changed their prices when factory incentives went up or down. Others in the study "adjusted" their prices when inventory levels changed, and some changed their prices weekly or even daily. So, if it's going to bother you that someone else may pay less than you for the same car, then make sure you get the best deal possible—not necessarily the first one mentioned.

How to Buy a "Value-Priced" Car for Less

For those who hate the new-car negotiating process, a specially-equipped "value-priced" deal is a lot better than paying close to retail under the old system. However, if you want to buy one of these cars and get an even better deal, assume that everything is negotiable and make a written offer for a lower price. Even though the salesman may claim that their prices are not negotiable, insist that he write up your (lower) offer and present it to the manager. And mention that if they turn it down, you'll make the same offer at all of their competitors. (See Chapter 12 for more negotiating tips.) Better yet, just use the CarBargains car buying service.

10

Timing is Everything: When to Buy

When it comes to getting the lowest price on a new car, *timing is everything*. If you're in the right place at the right time, you can get a great deal; show up too early or too late, and you'll pay more—sometimes a lot more.

Buying Too Soon

The new car market is a perfect illustration for the law of supply and demand: Whenever a dealer has more buyers than cars, everyone pays retail (or more). Two recent examples of this were the Mazda Miata and the Dodge Viper, both arriving with much publicity and little inventory. The initial buyers of those cars wanted them so badly that some paid $5,000 (or more) over sticker, just to be the first one on their block with that particular car. In the case of the Miata, thousands more became available within a year, and anyone could eventually buy one for sticker or less.

Automakers will hate me for saying this, but my best advice for car buyers is to avoid the initial introduction of any new model. First, new models almost always have more problems than models that have been out for a while. (So let them work the bugs out on someone else's car.) Second, you'll rarely be offered any kind of rebate or discounted price during the first few months of a new model introduction because the supply of cars is usually rather limited.

Later in the year, however, discounts often become available as the supply increases, and if the new model isn't selling very well, the factory may come out with rebates and other incentives. (This sometimes happens within 2 to 3 months if the factory was too optimistic in estimating sales.)

Factory Rebates & Incentives

Factory rebates and other incentives are just disguised price cuts that are used to increase sales when things get slow. Automakers hate to use rebates because they cut into their profits, but since buyers seem to stay away when no rebates are offered, it looks like they're saying that the cars are overpriced. So dealers cut their prices (with rebates) and buyers return to the showrooms.

Buyers need to use a service like Fighting Chance (see Chapter 11) to find out what incentives are available and when they expire. Incentive programs come and go, so if they don't have one right now on the car you want, it might be worth it to wait a month or two in case one comes along. (Don't bother waiting if you're trying to buy a real hot-selling model—they don't offer incentives on those.)

Some dealer incentives are based on volume, which means that the more cars they sell, the higher the incentive amount on every car sold during the program. *This type of incentive can give a dealer a good reason to sell you a car at a little-or-no-profit price*, because one more sale could end up generating thousands of extra incentive dollars for the dealership. The best time to buy a car that has a volume incentive is right before the program ends, within the last few days.

Sales Goals, Quotas & Little-or-No-Profit Deals

Before a salesman will consider selling a car for little-or-no profit, he has to have a real good reason, and that's where sales goals come into play. Most salesmen work on commission and will be affected by some type of a *monthly* goal or quota.

The benefits of meeting a sales goal can range anywhere from keeping his job to winning an expensive vacation trip, or getting paid a higher percentage on all the cars he sold during that month. Obviously, if your sale is the one that "puts him over the top," he will benefit greatly even though the deal has little-or-no profit in it for the dealership.

The whole sales department may also have monthly goals that could encourage the sales manager to approve several low-profit deals at the end of the month in order to make the final numbers higher. And since most incentive programs also expire around the end of the month, the last few days of the month are often a good time to get the lowest price on a car. (Just be sure to check the expiration dates of any incentive programs before deciding when to buy.)

Year-End Clearance Sales: Buying Last Year's Model

Some car buyers like to wait until the new models arrive, then they purchase last year's model during a dealer's "big year-end sale." While it is true that they are getting a brand new car at a reduced price, they're also buying a car that is already one year old and has probably depreciated several thousand dollars before they even get to drive it home. If that fact doesn't bother you, and you still prefer to buy last year's model, there are a few things you should know before buying one.

The best year-end deals can usually be found on cars that have some sort of manufacturer's "carryover allowance," which is an incentive the dealer receives for sales of previous-year-model vehicles after the newer models come out. Why do they do this? Because the automakers know that a dealer who is stuck with a lot of cars from the previous year will not order as many new models as they would like.

General Motors and Ford used to have carryover allowances that were 5% of MSRP, but those have been discontinued. Instead, both companies now use various incentives that are created for slow-moving models. The new incentives could be in the form of factory-to-dealer cash, customer rebates, below-market financing, or any combination of these items.

Ford's new carryover allowance could be anywhere from 2.5% to 7.5% of the MSRP, depending on the popularity of the vehicle and the amount of inventory left over. Incentives on leftover imports are usually specific dollar amounts, which could be as much as $6,000 to $10,000 on a luxury model.

You may not be able to find out about each and every carryover allowance. However, as a "smart shopper" who has done his homework (starting with this book, then the resources listed in Chapter 11), you should know about most of the incentives when you're ready to buy because you'll have a copy of *CarDeals*.

Here's an example of how a carryover allowance can affect the dealer's cost on a leftover new vehicle: On a car that retails for $20,000, the dealer might get a factory-to-dealer incentive of $2,000 along with the usual holdback (3%, or $600), adding up to $2,600 off the dealer's cost. (Don't forget—none of this will show up on the factory invoice.) Subtract the $2,600 from the typical factory invoice of $18,000 on our $20,000 car, and you'll see that the dealer's real cost is now only $15,400.

Now the dealer may not be willing to sell the car at his cost, but keep in mind that it is last year's model—and he's paying the bank interest on the car for as long as it sits on his lot. So, if he can't find another buyer at that price, he'll be forced to sell it below cost. Offer to buy it for his actual cost ($15,400 in our example) and see what happens. If that doesn't work, offer to let him keep some (or all) of the holdback money, which means raising your offer to $15,700 or $16,000.

Don't go much higher than real cost plus holdback, or you'll end up paying more than the car is worth. Remember—it's already a year old, so it's depreciated several thousand dollars. And it was only worth about $18,000 when it was a new model, because that's the amount that a "smart shopper" would have paid for it then.

As you can see, there is the possibility of significant discounts on year-end models, so make sure you receive them if you plan on buying a car this way. Don't settle for less, or you'll end up losing money when you sell the car or trade it in a few years later. Why? Because three or four years from now, a 2001 model will be worth about $1,500 to $2,000 more than a 2000 model. So if you can't buy the 2000 model for at least $1,500 less than the 2001 model, you're better off buying the newer one.

The Law of Supply and Demand: Use It to Your Advantage

How the law of supply and demand affects the sale of cars is fairly simple: 1) When there are more buyers than cars, prices go up, and 2) When there are more cars than buyers, prices go down. The secret to getting the best deal is to buy during the second market condition. As long as you don't have to buy that car immediately, you can always wait until the market favors you rather than the dealer. Also, by shopping around and making dealers compete for your business, you're helping to create favorable market conditions for yourself.

Here's how to tip the scales in your favor: Go to the dealer to buy your car when business is so slow that they'll be desperate to make a sale. The busiest days at car dealers are usually Saturday, Sunday, during big advertised sales and when the weather is nice. Instead, go on a weekday, around holidays like Christmas and Easter, when the weather is bad, and if you really want to see empty showrooms, go during the Superbowl.

11

Homework for Car Buyers

An impulsive or emotional shopper always ends up with the worst deal (or a bad case of "buyer's remorse") so avoid that mistake by taking the time to become a cool, calm, educated buyer. Promise yourself that the purpose of your first dealer visits will be *to look at everything and buy nothing.* Don't bring your checkbook or the title to your car, and don't agree to buy (or lease) anything—no matter how good it looks or sounds.

When you are visiting dealerships, salesmen will swarm around you even though you tell them you're "just looking." Tell them you're not going to buy anything for three or four weeks and they'll usually disappear, allowing you to take your time looking at different models. Collect brochures and other information, and don't be afraid to ask questions. Then go home—in your old car.

After visiting dealers to see which cars you like (and can afford), the next step is to research those models to see what kind of ratings they have, and also to see if they have any "twins or cousins" that may be less expensive.

If you're leasing, you should still research a vehicle's track record for safety, repairs, fuel economy, insurance cost and future resale value. Why? Even though you probably won't be interested in keeping the vehicle after the lease ends (otherwise you would be buying, not leasing), any one of these items has the potential to ruin your new car experience.

Following a brief explanation of these important items (and a few other things you should know), you'll find a resource section containing the best sources I've found for the information you need to get a great deal.

Safety

Safety is always ranked by consumers as an important feature on a new car, but all cars don't offer the same crash protection, so how can shoppers tell which ones are safer? Of course, you could ask the salespeople, but do you really think they'll tell you that a competitor's cars have better safety ratings? (Probably not.) Fortunately, there are a number of organizations and publications that provide safety ratings for all the new cars every year.

Repair History

Be sure to include a vehicle's repair history on your list of things to consider. There are significant differences in quality from one car to the next, so don't assume that your car is going to be trouble-free just because it's new. And even though you may be leasing, you'll still have to pay for maintenance and repairs to keep the vehicle in good condition. If you don't, you'll be hit with a hefty penalty when you turn the vehicle in.

Checking the repair history becomes even more important if you're considering a used car lease. Before a three-year-old vehicle ends up on a used car lot, its original factory warranty will usually have expired. And the warranty on a two-year-old car might only be good for another six months (or less) if the previous owner drove at least 15,000 miles per year. Since most used cars are sold or leased without any kind of warranty, choosing the wrong car can turn out to be an expensive mistake.

Fuel Economy

Unfortunately, the cars with the best fuel economy ratings are usually the smallest and lightest models, which means they won't do very well in an accident with a larger car. (Sorry, that's physics.) Also, the most miserly vehicles are usually the ones with the smallest engines and the fewest luxury features (like air conditioning). For most people, some fuel economy will be sacrificed to gain more safety, horsepower and/or accessories.

Insurance Cost

This item is frequently overlooked until after the new car is driven home. Of course, by that time it's too late to pick another car because the insurance is going to cost too much. Rates can vary dramatically from one model to another, so be sure to call your agent for a quote *before* you make the final decision. And don't assume you'll automatically be covered when you get a new car—let your agent know in advance when you plan on taking delivery.

A warning for new lease customers: Leases usually require higher liability coverage ($300,000) than you may normally carry, so be sure to find out what the insurance costs are going to be before signing a lease contract. And since you'll be getting a new vehicle every two or three years, your insurance payments will always be high. In states that have high insurance rates, this requirement can significantly increase the cost of driving a new car.

Depreciation (Future Resale Value)

Depreciation should be an important consideration when deciding which car to buy or lease. Some models can lose over 60% of their value (starting from MSRP) in the first 36 months, while others may only lose 40%. Since depreciation is usually the largest part of a monthly lease payment, choosing a model with good resale value should make it easier to negotiate lower payments.

Some vehicles have poor resale value because they have a history of spending too much time in the repair shop, so keep this in mind if you're tempted to lease or buy one anyway. Even on a three-year lease, you could easily run out of warranty before the lease is up (by driving over 12,000 miles per year), leaving you with repair bills on a car you don't own. To avoid this, check the repair history before signing any contracts.

Twins & Cousins

"Twins and cousins" are similar vehicles that are sold under different names. These cars usually have the same basic body style, engine and drivetrain. In many cases, the only differences are in trim, levels of luxury and/or which features are standard equipment. However, there can be significant differences in price, so you may be able to save money by purchasing the less expensive twin. (Example: Toyota Corolla and Chevrolet Prizm)

Dealer Cost Information

Whether you're buying or leasing, you need to know the dealer's real cost on a vehicle to get the best deal (and to figure out how much your lease payments should be). The "factory invoice" or "dealer invoice" figure doesn't tell the whole story; you also need up-to-date information on any factory-to-dealer incentives, allowances and hold-back money. (Be sure to read Chapters 3 and 12 for more on dealer cost and how to negotiate.)

Using a Car Buying Service

For those who hate the whole negotiating process (and would normally settle for little-or-no discount off the sticker price), I recommend using a new-car buying service. If you're leasing the vehicle, you can use their discounted price as the cap cost. (See Chapter 13 for more information.)

RESOURCES

Published Ratings

Consumer Reports, Annual Auto Issue (April)
****Most comprehensive data on repair histories
****Excellent used car reliability reports
    Also—new car facts, safety & reliability ratings,
        depreciation information

The Car Book, by Jack Gillis
****Most comprehensive safety data & ratings
    Other ratings: fuel economy, maintenance costs,
        warranties, tires
    New car facts, EPA mileage figures & much more

Kiplinger's New Car Buyer's Guide
****Excellent data on resale values & insurance costs
    Plus data on mileage, interior/cargo space & more

Books: Retail & Dealer Invoice Prices

1) *Edmund's New Car Prices*
2) *Pace Buyer's Guides, New Car Prices*
(Available in most bookstores)

Books: Used Car Prices

1) *Edmund's Used Car Prices*
2) *Kelley Blue Book/Used Car Guide, Consumer Edition*
(Available in most bookstores)

New-Car Buying & Leasing Information

FIGHTING CHANCE
5318 East 2nd Street, PMB 242
Long Beach, CA 90803
(800) 288-1134
(562) 433-8489

**** Four stars!
Fighting Chance is the best new-car information service
I've found, providing more insight and negotiating leverage than any other. They give you the retail, invoice and
holdback figures on the model (and options) of your

choice, plus a *CarDeals* report on dealer and customer in-centives for all vehicles, so you'll know which models are being secretly discounted.

Their package includes a "Big Picture" analysis for your make, providing the most recent sales and inventory data and telling you how much (or how little) other in-formed buyers have recently paid for your chosen vehi-cle. In addition, they provide several strategies to help you get the best possible deal, one of which shows you how to do all your negotiating painlessly by fax, without walking into a single car store. They also help their cus-tomers figure lease payments. One price covers the cur-rent and previous year's models. The cost for the first car is $24.95, additional cars are $8.00 each.

Leasing Guides/Software

CHART Software
430 Rio Casa Dr. N.
Indialantic, FL 32903
(800) 418-8450
(321) 773-7686

**** Four stars!
Expert Lease Pro is a great program. I use it to analyze leases for court cases and TV undercover investigations. Chart Software now offers two products/services:
1) Expert Lease Pro Software. This easy-to-use program can save you money on your next vehicle by giving you the tools to calculate lease and loan payments, perform lease/buy comparisons, compare leases and structure your own lease deals. Expert Lease Pro is great at uncovering hidden charges, APR lies and other leasing scams, and it comes with an outstanding data package that includes in-voice and MSRP prices for all new vehicles, *Automotive*

Lease Guide and *Black Book* residuals, and the *CarDeals* Rebate/Incentive report. With Expert Lease Pro you can take your laptop computer to the dealer and analyze their leasing deals on the spot! Featured in *Money Magazine, Smart Money, Kiplinger's Personal Finance Magazine, Home PC* and many others. Includes free use of Chart Software's Leasing Hot Line service (see below) where customers can get expert leasing advice via their toll-free number. Cost: $69.95.

2) Leasing Hot Line Service. This new service puts you in touch with a live expert via toll-free number. With the Leasing Hot Line, you can speak with an expert who will perform a 5-point analysis of your lease, point out any problems and answer your questions. This service is perfect for those preparing to lease as well as those with the next-day "lessor's remorse." The cost is $25 for the first 20 minutes plus $1 per additional minute. (Typical charge is $30 to $35.)

New-Car Buying Services

CarBargains
733 15th Street NW, Suite 820
Washington, DC 20005
(800) 475-7283
(202) 393-7610

**** Four stars!
CarBargains is the best new-car buying service I've seen. They promise to get you a lower price than you can get on your own, or your money back. You can also use their "purchase" bids to get a lower cap cost on a lease, which should result in lower payments. (Cost: $165)

CarBargains can also provide buyers with names of dealers promising to sell factory-sponsored service contracts (extended warranties) for $50 over cost. See Chapter 13 for more information.

Internet Resources at CarInfo.com

Be sure to visit our Web site, "CarInfo.com," for links to these (and other) great car-buying & leasing resources. Look for "$$ Saving Tips." This site also has the latest car-related consumer protection information. Tell your friends about it! (www.carinfo.com)

Twins & Cousins

GENERAL MOTORS (and partners):
Buick LeSabre/Buick Park Avenue/Pontiac Bonneville/
    Oldsmobile Aurora
Cadillac Seville/Cadillac Eldorado
Chevrolet Astro/GMC Safari vans
Chevrolet Blazer/GMC Jimmy/GMC Envoy/Oldsmobile
    Bravada
Chevrolet Camaro/Pontiac Firebird
Chevrolet Cavalier/Pontiac Sunfire
Chevrolet Express/GMC Savana vans
Chevrolet Impala/Monte Carlo
Buick Century/Buick Regal/Oldsmobile Intrigue/Pontiac
    Grand Prix
Chevrolet Metro/Suzuki Swift
Chevrolet Prizm/Toyota Corolla
Chevrolet S-Series/GMC Sonoma/Isuzu Hombre pickups
Chevrolet Silverado/GMC Sierra pickups
Chevrolet Suburban/GMC Yukon XL
Chevrolet Tahoe/GMC Yukon/GMC Denali/Cadillac
    Escalade
Chevrolet Venture/Oldsmobile Silhouette/Pontiac
    Montana minivans

Oldsmobile Alero/Pontiac Grand Am
Chevrolet Tracker/Suzuki Vitara/Grand Vitara
Pontiac Aztek/Buick Rendezvous

DAIMLERCHRYSLER:
Chrysler Concorde/Dodge Intrepid/Chrysler LHS/
    Chrysler 300M
Chrysler Sebring Sedan/Dodge Stratus
Chrysler Sebring Coupe/Dodge Stratus Coupe
Dodge Caravan/Chrysler Voyager/Chrysler Town &
    Country minivans

FORD (and partners):
Ford Contour/Mercury Mystique
Ford Crown Victoria/Mercury Grand Marquis
Ford Expedition/Lincoln Navigator
Ford Explorer/Mercury Mountaineer
Ford Ranger/Mazda B-Series pickups
Ford Taurus/Mercury Sable
Mercury Villager/Nissan Quest
    (both will be discontinued in 2001)
Ford Escape/Mazda Tribute
Lincoln LS/Jaguar S-Type

OTHERS:
Honda Passport/Isuzu Rodeo
Honda Accord/Acura TL/Acura CL
Honda Civic/Acura Integra
Nissan Maxima/Infiniti I30
Nissan Pathfinder/Infiniti QX4
Toyota Camry V6 XLE/Lexus ES 300
Toyota Land Cruiser/Lexus LX 470
Toyota Highlander/Lexus RX 300
Volkswagen Passat/Audi A4
Kia Sephia/Kia Spectra

12

How to Negotiate

If you skipped the first part of the book, you need to go back—this chapter is only for knowledgeable buyers who have done their homework and understand the business. By this time, you should know all about true dealer's cost and the numerous tricks salesmen use to get more of your money. You've thoroughly researched the model you want, including its mechanical and safety track records, you have a pre-approved car loan from the lender of your choice, and you've figured out a low-profit target price.

Before you start negotiating in person, there's a great strategy that's worth trying: "bidding by mail." The lowest bid can then be used to negotiate a better price with another dealer, or if it's the best deal you can find, use it to buy your new car or truck.

Bidding by Mail (or Fax)

In "bidding by mail," you get a number of dealers to make blind bids on a new car, without you being there. This has two big advantages: 1) They know that you will buy somewhere else if their bid isn't the lowest, and 2) Since you're not there, they can't use any of their tricks to get more money out of you.

Make a list of all the dealers you would be willing to buy from, then call them on the phone to get the names of their fleet managers along with their mailing addresses (or fax numbers). If a dealer doesn't have a fleet manager, get the name of the sales manager instead.

Draft a convincing letter to be sent to all the fleet managers on your list. The letters should be identical with the exception of the manager/dealer identification, and they must communicate that you are a serious and knowledgeable buyer.

In the letter, state that you are going to buy a specific model new vehicle, listing the color and any options, then ask them to quote you their best price. Mention that you are also getting quotes from other dealers in your area and the one with the lowest quote gets your business. Also mention that you have a pre-approved loan, but would be willing to consider any special factory financing that may be available.

Let them know you're aware of the dealer invoice and any factory-to-dealer incentives, so you expect the most competitive bids to be far below MSRP. Remind them to leave the customer rebate money (if applicable) out of their quotes; that money belongs to the buyer, so don't let the dealers use it to make their bids look better than they really are.

Be sure to mention that you do not want anything added to the car that's not factory-installed, especially paint sealer, fabric protection, undercoating, alarm system, etc. (Optional: If they can provide you with a factory-backed extended warranty at a *reasonable* price, you may be interested.) Ask them to include and itemize all charges in their quotes.

Your letter should have your name and address, both home and work phone numbers, and a fax number if you have one. Close with the statement that you will be making a final decision in two weeks, so you will assume that dealers who fail to respond by then are not interested. Thank them in advance, sign your name, mail the letters, and wait for the response! (If you can fax the letters instead of mailing them, this whole process may only take one week.)

Some dealers won't respond to this approach because they would rather have the "home court advantage," so be sure to send out at least four or five letters. If any of the dealers try to get you to come in before quoting a firm price (in writing), tell them you're not interested in doing business that way.

Negotiating in Person

Your overall negotiating strategy is to appear to be a serious, well-informed, unemotional buyer who has no preference for one dealer over another when it comes to purchasing a new car. If a salesman can tell that you're hopelessly in love with a car on his lot (or that you have some reason for not doing business with his competitors), you won't get the best possible deal, so find a way to conceal those emotions.

When you're ready to start negotiating, pick *at least* two or three dealerships you will give initial offers to, then gather your car information (vehicle worksheet, dealer invoice and incentive figures, etc.) to take with you. Your goal is to deal directly with a manager so you can get a "house sale" without any commission being paid to a salesman.

Call ahead to make an appointment. Try to meet with the fleet manager first, but if they won't let you, ask for the sales manager instead. Should they refuse to let you deal with a manager, tell them you are going to buy a car somewhere else, then call the next dealer on your list. Only deal with a salesman as a last resort: Since his commission is a percentage of the profit, he normally won't be interested in a low-profit sale.

Tell the manager/salesman you have decided which car to buy and you are prepared to make an offer. Refuse to discuss any trade-in at this time. When he asks how you are going to pay for the car, tell him you have a pre-approved loan, but you are open to other financing options. Don't give him your driver's license or Social Security number, unless you want him to run a quick credit check. (They do that so they'll know how much of a monthly payment you can afford, then they'll try every trick in the book to charge you as much as you can afford.) Don't fall for it; just tell them it isn't necessary— your credit is good.

Don't show all your cards at once; if you tell him up front that you know all their tricks so he's not going to be able to rip you off, you'll probably make him so mad that you'll never be able to buy a car from him at a reasonable price. Let him think he has the advantage, even though the advantage will be yours if you know the dealer's cost and their tricks. If he thinks they might finance your new car, you may get a better price, so tell him you'll be willing to discuss financing *after* you've agreed on price.

Use the same strategy for any trade-in: Tell him you'll discuss it afterwards, but count on selling your old car yourself, knowing that a dealer is not going to pay more than wholesale (if that much) unless he's made a fortune on your new car.

Whatever you do, don't give them your old car keys or a "good faith" deposit before you've agreed on a price. An unscrupulous dealer will just use those to hold you hostage while they try to wear you down, claiming that someone has misplaced them so you can't leave. A deposit is only necessary *after* your offer is accepted and you have a written contract signed by the manager.

Your Initial Offer

Your initial offer should be high enough to contain a minimal profit for the dealer. If it doesn't, they'll think that you have no idea what their cost is and your bid was just a wild guess. Make a written offer to purchase at the dealer invoice price *minus* any other factory-to-dealer incentives. Let the dealer keep the holdback money as his profit.

The following example would leave a $630 profit for the dealer, assuming a 3% holdback, $1,000 factory-to-dealer incentive, and a purchase price of $17,500.

Vehicle w/options	MSRP	$21,000
Dealer invoice		$18,500
Minus dealer incentive		-1,000
Your initial offer		$17,500

You should try to get most of the incentive money if there's a factory-to-dealer cash incentive involved, which means you'll be buying for hundreds (or thousands) of dollars below the dealer invoice. Settle for half of the incentive money *later*, if that's the best you can do.

Depending on the MSRP and the holdback percentage, the dealer's profit on your initial offer would be roughly $350-700. They would love to make more, but many dealers will take a low-profit deal like this. After all, a low-profit deal is better than no deal at all. (And a no-profit deal could end up making them money on other cars they sell if your car is part of a volume-based incentive program.)

After you've presented your initial offer, the manager/salesman will probably say that they can't possibly sell the car for that price because it's below their cost. (If you are dealing with a salesman, he may not know what the dealer's cost is.) Now's the time to pull out your printout from Fighting Chance and show him that you know exactly what their cost is—it's less than your offer.

When you do this, don't have a smirk on your face or a cocky attitude, just calmly show him what the dealer's cost is, including the holdback and any factory incentives. Be prepared for him to challenge your numbers. When he does, calmly suggest that he get the dealer invoice to see if the numbers are correct. Then insist that your offer be seriously considered.

If the salesman says he has to present the offer to his boss, tell him that you have another appointment so you can only wait ten minutes for him to return with their answer. Also tell him that he has your best offer for that day, and if they reject it, you will be leaving immediately to make the same offer at three or four other dealers. Then wait for their response—but only for ten minutes. When their time is up, leave the dealership.

Unless it's your lucky day, they probably won't accept your initial offer without your walking out first. (That's OK, it's all part of the plan.) Each time one of your offers is rejected, tell them to give you a signed, written quote of the lowest price they would take, then walk out.

When you have their counteroffer (or their ten minutes are up because they're stalling), leave the dealership immediately and repeat the process at the next dealer on your list. Continue making the same initial offer until one of the dealers agrees to sell at your price or you've run out of dealers. Do not—under any circumstances—increase your initial offer on the first day until you've presented it to all of the dealers on your list.

Incidentally, if anyone refuses to negotiate on your terms (including a refusal to quote you their "best price"), tell them you're sure you can find a dealer who will, then thank them for their time and leave. Be polite, because you want them to change their mind and call you back.

Your Best Weapon: Walking Out

Remember that your best negotiating weapon is your ability (and willingness) to walk out after a dealer rejects your offer, instead of staying to negotiate further. If you don't walk out, the salesman will assume that he hasn't heard your best offer yet, so he won't accept a low bid.

You might have to make two offers at the same dealership before you get a good deal, and you'll have to walk out after the dealers turn down each of your offers to convince them that they're not going to get any more money out of you. Yes, this might take several visits to the same dealer, but if each visit is a polite "take-it-or-leave-it" offer (instead of a three- or four-hour battle with a salesman), it won't take that much time. *This is the only way to get the best deal on a car.*

What usually happens when you walk out (after they reject your offer) is that they will eventually run after you, often waiting until you're back in your car to see if you're bluffing. To get you back inside, they'll say anything. ("Mr. Smith, let me present your offer to my boss one more time. Since it's the end of the day, I'm sure he will accept it.") They won't let you get away if they know you're a serious buyer; their goal is to get you back inside so they can sell you a car—for more money.

When they try this, tell them you're not going back inside unless they're ready to accept your offer. If necessary, give them your phone number and tell them to call you when they're serious about selling the car. Remind them that you are going to several other dealers to make the same offer, then leave.

Your Revised Target Price

Assuming that none of your initial offers were accepted, you should now have a number of bids (written counteroffers) from the dealers you visited. The next step is to figure out a new target price for your second written offer, one that will be harder for dealers to reject.

Your new offering price should be about $200 to $300 more than your original offer. On lower-priced cars (with an MSRP of $9,000 to $12,000), an additional $200 is a substantial increase that should be tempting to some dealers, since those vehicles have a lower profit margin to begin with. On mid-sized (and larger) cars, you might have to increase your original offer by $250 to $300 to make it attractive.

If there is a factory-to-dealer incentive, your new target price could still be hundreds (or thousands) below dealer invoice; if no dealer incentive exists, your new bid may be 1-2% over invoice. *Do not offer more than 2% over dealer invoice on your second bid.*

Before you present your second offer, go over the written counteroffers you received. Wait until at least four or five days have gone by since your initial offer, then phone all of the dealers on your list and ask if they have reconsidered your offer. Tell the dealers with the higher bids what the low bid was, then ask if they will beat that bid to sell you the car. They probably won't offer to beat it by more than a token amount (maybe as little as $25 or $50), but that's OK because you're not going to offer that much—unless a new bid is so close to your revised target price that you're willing to accept it. *Don't make any commitments at this time.* Tell them you will think it over and call them back when you're ready.

Use the information gained from the phone calls to "fine-tune" your new target price. If you get several bids that are close to your new target price, lower it. For example, if several dealers say they'll sell for $400 more than your initial offer, you know you're getting close to a figure that will be tempting, so only increase your offering price $200 (instead of $300).

Your Second Offer

Present the second offer in the same manner as the first, asking for a written counteroffer if your offer is rejected. Remind them that you will be making the same offer at several other dealers, then leave. Don't let them talk you into raising your offer during that visit—there's a much better chance that they'll compromise first if you walk out after they reject your offer. Be sure to present your second offer to all of the dealers on your list before you consider increasing your bid (unless one of them accepts your offer, in which case you're done).

As you begin to offer dealers $500 to $800 over their true cost—*not invoice*—some of them will worry that one of the others might accept your offer if they turn you down, so don't be too quick to raise your second offer until a week has gone by and you don't have any takers. If that happens, call the dealers back and ask if they've reconsidered your offer.

Unless you're in a seller's market (which is rare), you should be able to find a dealer who's tempted by one of your offers. In a seller's market, when it's more difficult for buyers to find drastically-reduced prices, you may end up paying 3% to 4% over dealer invoice—especially if you're not willing to wait several months for another incentive program to come along.

If you make it through your whole dealer list with two offers, resulting in no deals or good counteroffers, you might want to consider using CarBargains' car buying service. This is especially true if your second offer was 2% over dealer invoice. (Most of the dealer bids that CarBargains gets for its customers are *at invoice or less*. See Chapter 13 for more information.)

Should you decide against using a buying service after your second offers are rejected, raise your offering price by $200 (or $100 to $150 on lower-priced cars) and repeat the process. If your new price is now around 4% over dealer invoice and you can't find any takers, you might want to reevaluate the timing of your offers—it could be worthwhile to wait a month or two until incentives change or one of the dealers is more motivated to sell. *Paying much more than 4% over invoice is not a bargain on most cars.*

The "Little-or-No Profit" Deal

For those shrewd negotiators (and thrifty shoppers) who want to buy a new car for the absolute, rock-bottom, lowest price anyone will ever get, and don't care how many visits or how much time it takes to get what they want, here's how to negotiate a "little-or-no profit" deal on a new car. Keep in mind that this is not easy to do and your success will depend on persistence, timing, luck, and finding a desperate salesman or dealer. Only a small percentage of buyers will be able to pull this off.

Use the negotiating process outlined in this chapter, but start with a target price that contains no profit for the dealer. This means that you will start with the dealer invoice price, then subtract all factory-to-dealer incentives and holdback money to arrive at "true dealer cost" for that vehicle. Your target price could be hundreds or thousands below dealer invoice, depending on the amount of dealer incentive. (Accurate information on dealer cost is crucial when using this strategy, so be sure to use Fighting Chance for invoice and incentive information. See Chapter 11.)

The following example shows how far below MSRP a "no-profit" bid can be. Dealer holdback is 3% of the list price and there is a $1,000 factory-to-dealer incentive.

Vehicle w/options	MSRP	$21,000
Dealer invoice		$18,500
Minus dealer holdback		-630
Minus dealer incentive		-1,000
Your initial offer		$16,870

Timing is the key ingredient of this strategy—you must present your "no-profit" bid to the right person at the right time. An offer like this that helps a salesman or manager meet a quota (or win a contest) may be tempting if it's presented at the end of the month, because quotas and contests are often based on monthly sales. A no-profit sale on a vehicle that's part of a volume-based factory-to-dealer incentive program can generate considerable profits for a dealer, so present these offers near the end of the incentive program.

Present your "no-profit" bid to as many dealers as you can until your offer is accepted or you run out of dealers.

Be sure to walk out after each bid is rejected, and don't increase your offering price until after your bid is presented and rejected by all of the dealers on your list.

If you have to raise your bid after the first round because all of the dealers rejected it, only increase your offer by $200 for the second round, making it a "$200 profit" deal.

The "Year-end Clearance Sale"

Should you decide to visit one of those big year-end clearance sales to find a "great deal" on a brand new car that's now last year's model, be sure to use the "little-or-no profit" strategy when making an offer. Even though these cars have no miles on them, they're still one year old and depreciation has reduced their market value by at least 20%. Try not to pay much more than the dealer's true cost on one of these vehicles, because the car may not even be worth that much.

The following example includes a 3% dealer holdback based on MSRP and a 5% dealer (carryover) incentive because the car is left over from last year. Notice that the dealer's true cost (your initial offer) is slighter higher than the estimated market value of the vehicle.

<u>Vehicle w/options</u>   MSRP   <u>$20,000</u>

Dealer invoice	$18,000
Minus dealer holdback	-600
Minus carryover	<u>-1,000</u>
Your initial offer	$16,400

<u>MSRP — 20% depreciation = market value</u>

$20,000   — $4,000   = $16,000

When You've Got a Deal

When you've reached an agreement on price, the dealer will probably want to discuss financing, trade-in and the usual array of "after-sell" rip-offs designed to increase his profit margin. If you've done your homework and you stand your ground, they won't be able to take advantage of you. This means you'll probably use your own lender, sell your own car, and refuse to pay for anything other than tax, license, destination charge and a minimal "doc fee" ($30 to $40).

Charges You Don't Have to Pay

Some common unnecessary, overpriced and/or worthless "second sticker" items added on by dealers: fabric protection, paint sealer, rustproofing/under-coating, pinstriping, car alarms, "special value packages," floor mats, "protection packages," etc. These are just "cash cows" for the dealer—don't pay for any of them.

If they claim that you have to pay for one or more items on the "second sticker" because they're already on the car, tell them to take those items off or get you another car without them. Just say that you don't want those things on your car and you're not going to pay for them. Let them know you'll cancel the purchase if they insist on charging you for unwanted "options." (See Chapter 5.)

Beware of charges for "dealer prep" and "national advertising." *Don't pay them.* Dealers are paid by the manufacturer for dealer preparation, so if you pay for it, they get paid twice. (This is obviously a very profitable rip-off, often adding about $200 to the dealer's pocket.) Advertising is a normal business expense that should not be added to a customer's final bill. (This rip-off is usually priced at 1% of the MSRP.)

Watch for items listed as "processing charges" or "closing costs." What they're trying to do here is make you pay for their employees handling the paperwork, a normal cost of doing business. A $10 or $20 fee may not be worth fighting over, but if the fee is $50 or more, you should refuse to pay it.

If the dealer is handling the financing, he'll probably try to sell you credit life or disability insurance. *Don't fall for this!* If you want the extra insurance (though you probably don't need it), you can always buy it from your own insurance agent for a lot less.

Everyone who buys a car will be told by the finance and insurance "specialist" that they should buy an extended warranty to protect themselves from expensive repair bills after the original warranty runs out. These high-profit warranties are always good for the dealer's bottom line, but not always good for the buyer; sometimes they are an absolute rip-off. Before you decide whether to buy an extended warranty or not, be sure to read Chapter 6.

Charges You Do Have to Pay

The list of items you do have to pay for is fairly short: the destination charge, sales tax, license/doc fees and the car itself. Everything else is optional.

One Last Note

Before you take delivery of your new car (or sign papers acknowledging delivery), be sure to give it a thorough inspection. You'll have a much better chance of getting things fixed to your satisfaction *before* you actually take delivery. (See Chapter 16.)

13

CarBargains:
A Shortcut to Savings

Some people just don't have the ability (or the desire) to do battle with car dealers, so arming them with industry secrets is not going to save them any money when they buy (or lease) a new car. So, should these people just resign themselves to paying hundreds or thousands more than someone else for the same car or truck? Absolutely not—they should use CarBargains!

CarBargains is a service provided by the Center for the Study of Services, a non-profit consumer group in Washington, DC. Unlike auto brokers and other car buying services that are "for-profit" and may be affiliated with specific dealers, CarBargains is completely independent and does not take any money from dealers for steering buyers toward a particular dealer. CarBargains shops many different dealers to get customers the best prices on new vehicles, and it's the best service that I've found.

Tests have been conducted by consumer magazines and TV news programs to compare the prices that major car-buying services can get. In a 1998 *Money Magazine* test of CarBargains and three large Internet buying services (Autobytel, AutoVantage and CarPoint), the lowest prices were obtained by CarBargains in nine out of ten comparisons. In this test, *Money* shopped for prices on two popular models (Ford Explorer and Toyota Camry) in five cities: Seattle, San Diego, Boston, New Orleans and Portland, Maine. After adding their $165 fee to the prices they obtained, CarBargains still beat the Internet services by margins of $400 to $800 per car.

In an earlier test of car-buying services by *ABC News 20/20*, CarBargains obtained significantly lower prices (on a Toyota Camry and a Ford Taurus) than four other services. The other services in this 1996 test were Price Costco, AutoVantage, Automobile Consumer Services and Sam's Club. CarBargains beat all of the other services by margins of $600 to $1,300 per car.

How does CarBargains keep getting lower prices than their competition? In most cases, it's because CarBargains is getting five competing quotes for each customer and the others are only getting a price from their one affiliated dealer in a particular area.

How CarBargains Works

CarBargains will make dealers compete with each other for your business, allowing you to avoid the unpleasant (and often costly) experience of negotiating on a new vehicle. They are so confident of their ability to get you the best possible deal that their service has a money-back guarantee: *If you are able to buy a car at a price lower then the best quote included in their report, without using their information, they will gladly refund your entire fee.*

To use CarBargains, call toll free (800) 475-7283. The fee for their service is $165 which can be paid by check or credit card. If you decide to order by mail, make your check payable to "CarBargains" and specify the year, make and model of the vehicle you wish to buy. Include a daytime phone number and mail your request to:

CarBargains
733 15th Street NW, Suite 820
Washington, DC 20005

The following is a brief description of how the CarBargains service works:

1. You tell them the year, make, model and style of the car or truck you wish to buy (for example, "a 2000 Honda Accord LX 4-Door Sedan").

2. Within two weeks, CarBargains will get at least five dealers in your area to bid against each other on the vehicle you requested. Each dealer will commit to a specific dollar amount above (or below) the "factory invoice" price of the vehicle.

3. You will receive a report that includes:

   • Dealer quote sheets showing how much above (or below) factory invoice cost each dealer has agreed to sell, and listing the names of the sales managers at each dealer responsible for the commitment.

   • Factory invoice cost information for your type of car

or truck, showing what all dealers pay for the base vehicle and for each possible option.

- Other useful information: on the value of your used car (based on a description you have given them), low-cost financing options, pros and cons of extended warranties/service contracts, how you may be able to get a service contract as good as your dealer offers at a substantially lower cost, etc.

4. You visit one or more of the dealers and—

- Look at the vehicles on the lot;
- Select the specific vehicle you want;
- Use the information they've sent you to determine the factory invoice cost of the vehicle you selected;
- See the sales manager listed on your report's dealer quote sheets and purchase the vehicle at the factory invoice cost plus (or minus) the amount agreed to by the dealer.
- If a vehicle with the options you want is not available on a dealer's lot, you can have the dealer order the vehicle (if available) from the factory, or from another dealer, at the agreed markup (or markdown) figure.

FREQUENTLY ASKED QUESTIONS

Can't I do this myself?

Dealers know that CarBargains' bidding is for real—they know they will actually get at least 5 quotes. In addition, they know that a consumer who has paid for the CarBargains service is almost certain to buy immediately from one of the quoting dealers, so refusing to quote means losing a sale. However, when you call for a bid, the dealer may not believe that you will bother to get bids elsewhere. Worse yet, dealers often refuse to bid over the phone with consumers, using lines such as, "shop around, then come on down—we'll beat anyone else's price." They don't usually take telephone shoppers seriously.

Dealers know that CarBargains will get bids from other dealers, so each dealership knows it will have to bid real low to have any chance of winning. They remind dealers of any ongoing factory-to-dealer incentive programs, manufacturer holdbacks, carryover allowances and other factors that give the dealer room to cut his price. Also, dealers know that if CarBargains doesn't get good prices locally, they will get quotes from dealers outside the area who will deliver new cars locally.

CarBargains is also a witness to the dealers' quotes; they get signed commitments by fax and dealers know they will follow up. On the other hand, if a customer gets a quote by phone, some dealers may feel they can back out without serious consequences.

The CarBargains staff are car-buying experts. They make sure all costs (advertising association fees, processing fees, dealer-installed options, etc.) are included in the dealers' bids, not added on later.

How close will the dealers be to my home?

CarBargains has a computer file of all dealers in the country. When you order their service, they identify dealers close to you and get them to bid. You can even have them include (or leave out) a dealer of your choice.

Will I still get a factory rebate?

Your CarBargains report will tell you whether the car you

are buying has a customer (cash) rebate. If it does, you can choose to keep the rebate money, or you can use it for part (or all) of the down payment.

Do I have to decide which options I want before calling CarBargains?

No. You only need to tell them the year, make, model and style of car you want. The dealers bid a specific dollar amount above (or below) the factory invoice price. Car-Bargains will send you a printout that lists the factory invoice prices for the base vehicle and for each available factory-installed option. This allows you to decide which options you want later, while still being able to figure out the total factory invoice amount.

Is CarBargains able to get any car at a discount price?

Almost—the only car that's *never* available at a discount is a Saturn. Certain models that are in short supply may sell at a premium for a brief period (like the first Mazda Miatas), but most cars and trucks are available somewhere at a dealer who's willing to sell at a substantial discount.

How much can CarBargains save me on popular models?

CarBargains consistently gets great prices for their customers. Results will vary depending on the time of year, whether any factory-to-dealer incentives are in effect, and from one region to another. In the past, there has usually been little discounting of new model-year vehicles in the first few months after introduction, but that appears to be changing due to increased competition. (Some brand-new models have recently sold at a discount.)

Examples of recent prices obtained by CarBargains:

	From Invoice/Sticker
2000 Nissan Altima GXE 4-Cyl	-$200/-$1817
2000 Mercury Cougar 3DR V6	+$100/-$1614
2000 Ford F-150 XLT 4WD	-$200/-$2991
2000 Chevy S-10 Ext. Cab LS	+$250/-$1898
2000 Chrysler Sebring JXi V6	-$300/-$2618
2000 Dodge Grand Caravan LE	+$100/-$2593
2000 Mazda Millenia S V6	+$100/-$2533
2000 Cadillac Escalade	-$1750/-$5524

The above numbers represent prices compared to the dealer invoice and the sticker price. Most of these vehicles had customer rebates that were not included in the above numbers, so actual discounts were often greater.

As is the case with many other products, car prices are usually determined by supply and demand. Some models are never sold below invoice; sometimes the best available price may, in fact, be the full "window sticker" price, which could be 5% to 23% above dealer invoice, depending on the model.

For consumers, the goal should be to find the best price that is available when they are ready to buy. The CarBargains service is designed to find that price by making car dealers bid for the consumer's business. It not only produces a great price, it also spares the consumer the hassles and high-pressure sales tactics often associated with buying a new car.

Note For Leasing Customers

Consumers can also use the CarBargains service to find a good "purchase" price, which they can then use for a discounted cap cost on a lease.

14

Auto Brokers, Car-Buying Services & Membership Clubs

A number of car-buying services have appeared on the national scene, taking advantage of consumers' distaste for negotiating with dealers. All of them promise substantial discounts on new cars and trucks (without the consumer doing any of the haggling) but results vary, sometimes dramatically. One service may be able to get a price that's hundreds less than the others and in some cases, a determined, knowledgeable consumer has negotiated a better price on his own than most of the services could get.

The following sections explain how the various services work, and why some work better than others. Potential problems associated with some services are also covered, and my personal recommendation is included.

Auto Brokers

Auto brokers and car-buying services both claim to save consumers big money on the purchase of a new vehicle, but there are major differences in how they operate and make their money. These differences are significant and could affect not only the price you pay for a car, but what kind of service you receive after the purchase.

There are some companies using the name "broker" when they are actually operating as a buying service (for example, Nationwide Auto Brokers). Sometimes the only way to tell is to ask whether they are actually "buying and selling" or just shopping for the best price. For the purpose of this discussion, an "auto broker" is a business that buys new cars from dealers to resell to consumers, and a "car-buying service" is a business that shops around for the best price, then refers customers to specific dealers to buy the cars.

Auto brokers have been around for a long time, but it doesn't look like they've captured much of the car-buying market. How they operate could be at least partially responsible for their lack of popularity. Brokers take orders from consumers, buy the cars from dealers (with the broker actually taking title to the vehicles), then resell the cars to consumers—after adding a markup, of course.

When using a broker, the customer is usually required to put up either a large non-refundable deposit or the full purchase price before the car is ordered, creating a huge risk should something go wrong. Some brokers have gotten into legal trouble for taking deposits, then failing to deliver the vehicles, causing some of their customers to lose large sums of money. For this reason, among others, I do not recommend the use of a true "broker." (They're also illegal in many states.)

Since brokers are not licensed to sell new cars, the broker actually becomes the "original owner" of the car, and the final customer is (legally) purchasing a "used" car. All original factory warranties do remain in effect for the final customer, though, and buyers can still get a "new car" loan rate.

Brokers usually buy from the same dealers, claiming to get low prices because of their "high volume." However, since they're not making a number of dealers compete with each other over every vehicle, it's doubtful that their prices are going to be the lowest available. Remember: It's competition that creates low prices, not "volume."

Instead of receiving a fixed payment for negotiating a purchase, brokers make differing amounts of money based on the "spread" between their cost on the car and what the customer pays for it. A broker's desire to make a bigger profit is in direct conflict with the consumer's desire to get the lowest possible price, and since a broker is actually taking title and delivery of every vehicle he handles, he would have to make more money on a car than a buying service that is just shopping for the best price.

Another drawback to using auto brokers concerns their taking title to a car before reselling it to the consumer, making the broker the "original owner" of record with the manufacturer (just as a leasing company would be). In some cases, this may result in poor service for a buyer who takes his car to a dealership that treats people better if they bought a car there, and worse yet, if the dealer resents the fact that they used an auto broker.

When ordering a new vehicle through a broker, you will have more leverage to get things fixed *before* you

147

take delivery. After all, the broker just ordered the car—he doesn't represent the manufacturer and he can't fix the car for you. You may be told, "Don't worry, let's just get all the paperwork done so you can take your new car home, then you'll have more time to look it over. Your local dealer will be glad to fix anything you find wrong, so there's no need to do that right now." (This may or may not be true.)

A potentially serious problem with being the "second owner" of a new car is that vehicle recall notices and other manufacturer communications are usually sent only to the original owner, so if they don't get forwarded, you may not find out that your car was recalled for a safety defect.

Car-Buying Services

A number of car-buying services have sprung up recently and are gaining in popularity. For a fee (anywhere from $49 to $295 or more), these services promise to save you big money on a new car by doing the negotiating. Some even offer a money-back guarantee that they can get you a better deal than you can get on your own.

Car-buying services differ from true "brokers" in that a buying service does not actually buy or sell cars; instead, they get competing bids from dealers on the car you want. When they're through collecting bids (usually from four or five dealers), they turn them over to you to decide which dealer you want to use. You can then buy from the one with the lowest bid or use that bid to negotiate a better price with the dealer of your choice. The bids are usually from local dealerships, unless you specify how far you're willing to drive to save more money.

All that's left for you to do after you've selected a dealer is to decide whether you want to arrange your own financing or use the dealer's financing. Then you simply go to the dealer to sign the papers and pick up your new car.

There are many advantages to using a car-buying service over an auto broker. Most people who use a buying service will end up getting their new car from a local dealership, so they should be treated just like anyone else who bought a car there if they need to go back later for service. Also, since no one else is first taking title to the car and reselling it, the consumer will be registered as the "original owner," ensuring that he will receive all recall notices and other factory correspondence pertaining to his car.

Since car-buying services are only shopping around for the best prices, their overhead should be lower than that of auto brokers who actually buy the cars and take possession. Brokers obviously need to make more money on each car to cover the additional costs.

All car-buying services are not alike. Some take money from dealers for steering customers their way (usually at least $200 per car), which not only increases the dealer's cost, but often the price to the customer as well. Buying services that charge the consumer less than $100 are usually being paid by dealers.

Some buying services protect their customers from "back-end sales" and some don't. If yours doesn't, you might be talked into buying some worthless and/or grossly overpriced services (like undercoating and extended warranties) when you go to pick up your car. Before you pay to use a buying service, ask how much information they provide regarding back-end sales in the finance and insurance office.

Another thing to watch out for at some car-buying services is the offer of a "discount coupon book" for auto repairs and services. (More on this later in the chapter.)

Warehouse Club Car-Buying Programs

Car-buying programs that are run by the discount warehouses typically have an agreement with only one dealership in each area for a particular type of vehicle, eliminating any competition between dealers for the same car. Members are guaranteed a price that is a specific dollar amount (usually $300 to $500) *above* the dealer invoice, even when there may be a dealer holdback and/or factory-to-dealer incentive that reduces the dealer's cost to $500 (or as much as $1,500) *below* invoice.

For example, the Price Club (now PriceCostco) Auto Buying Program for the San Francisco area was steering club members to a local Toyota dealer who had promised to sell Camrys for $399 *above* invoice. However, the Car-Bargains buying service obtained dealer bids for $600 *below* invoice for the same car, in the same area, at the same time. By making dealers compete for the business, CarBargains was able to get their customers prices that were $999 lower than Price Club on the same car.

Generally speaking, warehouse club car-buying programs are a lot better than paying retail, but a good buying service (or even a knowledgeable consumer) should be able to beat their prices.

Credit Union Car-Buying Programs

Many credit unions (and other groups) have arranged for their members to have access to some type of discount car-buying program. Some might use a local auto broker, others may use a buying service or program similar to the warehouse clubs.

The new-car prices that are obtained through some of these programs are not even as low as a knowledgeable consumer could get by negotiating on his own, so be sure to compare their prices with other services before making a commitment to use them.

Club Discount Coupon Books

Discount coupons have been used by many well-known auto repair companies to lure consumers into their shops. In too many cases, unsuspecting motorists have been sold unnecessary repairs by mechanics and/or service advisors who were paid a sales commission or were working under some type of sales quota. Contests have even been used to reward employees for selling more repairs than anyone else, a practice that encourages widespread fraud.

AutoVantage, a major car-buying service, has set up a membership club to save cardholders money on a variety of automotive services and repairs, through the use of a discount coupon book. While most of the businesses featured in their coupon books may have good reputations, AutoVantage has included several national auto repair companies that have been accused of fraudulent business practices as a result of undercover investigations and/or class-action lawsuits.

The AutoVantage coupon book provides discounts on services at Aamco Transmission Centers, Goodyear Auto Centers and Firestone stores. A number of Aamco, Goodyear and Firestone shops have been accused of fraudulent business practices after undercover investigations were done in the past.

AutoVantage also had Kmart Auto Centers and Midas Muffler & Brake Shops in their previous coupon books. (Kmart's repair shops were sold in 1995; they are now Penske Auto Centers.) In California, a number of Midas Muffler shops have been accused of fraudulent business practices after undercover investigations were done by state authorities and a Los Angeles TV station.

Goodyear (company-owned) Auto Centers and Kmart Auto Centers were both targets of nationwide class-action lawsuits over allegations of fraudulent practices in their repair shops. The two companies were accused of creating an environment that resulted in the sale of unnecessary repairs through the use of sales commissions, quotas and/or contests for the highest sales.

The complete stories of the undercover investigations mentioned above (and many more) are contained in my book, *What Auto Mechanics Don't Want You to Know.*

My Personal Recommendation

For those buyers who don't want to do battle with dealers, but would still like to save as much money as possible on a new car, I recommend using the CarBargains buying service. They consistently get lower prices than the other services, they're not paid by dealers, and they also provide other valuable money-saving advice for consumers. (See Chapter 13 for more information.)

15

Internet Car-Buying Secrets

According to recent news articles, 40% of new-car buyers are now using the Internet for part (or all) of their car-shopping process. Scores of automotive Web sites have popped up, with most offering "free price quotes," "dealer cost information," and "the lowest prices." Sounds great, doesn't it? Instead of haggling in person with a salesman over the price of a new car, you can just go online, find out the dealer's cost on that new car or truck, and get the lowest price. Then all you need to do is drive to a local dealer to sign a few papers and drive home in your new car. Some buying services will even deliver the paperwork (and the new car) to your home or office, so you won't have to see the dealer to finalize your purchase.

So, is it really that easy? Can you just "log on" and get the dealer's real cost on that new car, then get the lowest price without any haggling? Or are those claims just advertising hype from a different type of salesman? In most cases, it's just hype. Most Web-surfing buyers are not getting the dealer's real cost on a new car (they're just getting the invoice price), and they're not getting the lowest possible prices either. In fact, two recent surveys have now confirmed that car buyers are not finding great service, or the lowest prices, at Internet buying services.

In December of 1999, CNW Marketing announced the results of its survey of 1.1 million car buyers who had used Internet buying services. Their survey showed that the Internet services did not offer the lowest prices, and that their customers often paid more than car buyers who bought the old way, that is, haggling with dealers in their showrooms.

In March of 2000, *Consumer Reports* announced the results of its Internet car-buying study. The magazine had 1,056 people request quotes on six different vehicles from five major Internet car-buying sites. Responding dealers were supposed to be within 100 miles of the shopper, and they were to deliver the quotes within two business days.

According to *Consumer Reports,* shoppers did find a lot of useful information at the Internet car-buying sites, but their service was often poor: Quotes were often received for vehicles that did not match the exact vehicle in the request, and only 35% of the shoppers received their quotes within the two-day time limit. In addition, 22% of the shoppers were not given firm prices when they were initially contacted by dealers; they were instead told that they would have to visit the dealer.

In my own test of major Internet car-buying sites (in June of 2000), I got similar results: Some of the quotes that I received were on vehicles that did not match my request, and at least one of the quotes was admitted to be off by about $1200. (They said, "Sorry, but we forgot to include the extra charge for the automatic transmission you requested, and we forgot to include the destination charge.") One service didn't have a dealer in or near Sacramento, which has a metro-area population of over one million people. (Their dealer was about 70 miles away.) And some of the responses from dealers did not include price quotes. (In spite of the fact that my request contained my email address and daytime phone number, one email response from a dealer asked me to call him for a price quote.)

The evidence indicates that car buying on the Internet fails to live up to its advertising hype, but the Internet can be very useful in conducting all that research you'll have to do before you can get the best possible price on a new or used car. Like the car-buying sites, the research sites have their strengths and weaknesses. In some cases, there are a few things to watch out for.

Using the Internet for Research

Pros: Lots of free information, including prices on cars, loans, extended warranties and insurance, plus advice on car buying and leasing. You can get free quotes on new and used cars, and you can even apply for car loans and insurance online. Cons: Too much information. There are so many car-buying sites that it's not possible to visit all of them and read their material. To make matters worse, they're all claiming to have the best deals (which clearly isn't true), and some of their information has been found to be out-of-date, inaccurate and/or misleading. Some ads that are found in free research (and other large) sites are there because they offer more money to the site owner, not because they offer better deals to the consumer.

"Dealer Cost" vs. Dealer Invoice Information

A lot of the "dealer cost" information on the Internet is wrong, especially when the only number that is provided is the dealer invoice price. To arrive at an accurate dealer cost number, holdback and other factory-to-dealer incentives must be provided with the invoice price, and all of the numbers must be current.

Most sites don't provide all the information people need to figure out the real dealer cost on a car, and some that do have the right information don't update it often enough. Sites sometimes have MSRP, invoice and/or dealer incentive numbers that contradict the numbers found in other sites, making it difficult for consumers to know which numbers are accurate.

New Car "Fair Price" / "Target Price" Listings

Some sites may have a "fair price" or "target price" alongside the MSRP and the invoice price, with a notation that the fair price or target price is one that they have determined to be a good or fair price for dealers to sell the car at. Some even state that consumers should try to buy at those prices, adding that those prices include a "fair profit" for the dealer. (This practice has also been found in some printed price guides at bookstores.)

What these sites don't tell you is that smart shoppers (who do their homework and know how to negotiate) are often buying cars for less, sometimes much less, than their "fair price." For example, a recent "fair price" on a popular car was supposed to be $600 over invoice, but several dealers were quoting prices of $100 over invoice on the same car. Since some dealers are willing to sell for less, the "fair price" and "target price" listings should be ignored. Always try for the lowest possible price.

Free Price Quotes on New & Used Cars

There are a number of car-buying services that offer free price quotes on the Internet. They rarely quote really low prices, but since the services are free, get a lot of quotes anyway. (You can then use the quotes to negotiate better deals with other dealers.) Don't count on the services getting quotes from a number of dealers in your area (unless you're using a multiple quote service like the one in our site), because it's fairly common for one dealer to represent several different services. Most of the major services allow you to get the MSRP and invoice prices before you request a quote. However, none provide the holdback or other dealer incentive information, so you have to use other resources to learn the dealer's real cost.

Direct Car-Buying Services

Direct car-buying services will quote you a firm price on a new car directly, either online immediately or by email the next day. They claim that they can get you a great price on a new car without you visiting (or even talking to) a dealer. How? After you get a price quote, and give them a deposit, they'll buy the car from a dealer and sell it to you. They'll even deliver the vehicle to your home or office. Some of their prices are good, but some are higher than prices obtained through a free quote service or even by a smart shopper buying the old way (haggling).

The downside: Some automakers have been pressuring their dealers not to sell to direct car-buying services, using threats that dealers are risking the loss of rebate money—and their franchises—if they sell to Internet car brokers. Direct car-buying services have been selling thousands of cars every month. However, they've also been losing a lot of money, which has forced at least one of them to raise their prices. Taking all these factors into account, these services may not have much of a future.

Useful Research Sites

There are three car-buying research sites that offer a lot of useful information. The first is Edmunds, run by the publisher of *Edmunds New Car Prices* (sold in book-stores). It's got articles on buying and leasing, prices on new and used cars, plus dealer invoice, holdback and incentive information. (www.edmunds.com) The second is Kelley Blue Book, run by the publisher of the respected used-car price guides. Their site has prices on new and used cars, plus dealer invoice, but it lacks information on dealer holdback and incentives. (www.kbb.com) And the third is IntelliChoice, by the publisher of *The Complete Car Cost Guide*. Their site has articles on leasing as well as a listing of the lowest-cost manufacturers' lease deals. (www.intellichoice.com)

Conclusion

All things considered, Internet research is a great tool for car buyers, especially if they can figure out which information is trustworthy. To that end, be sure to visit our Web site, CarInfo.com (www.carinfo.com), for the best car-buying resources, money-saving tips and consumer protection information. You might even find some major news stories (about car dealers) that have been covered up by your local newspaper and/or TV station.

16

Your New Car: Taking Delivery

After all the negotiating is over and agreement has been reached on price and terms, there are still two things left to do before the dealer (and the salesman) can get paid—you have to sign the loan papers (or pay cash), and you have to sign the delivery receipt acknowledging that you have taken possession of your new car. Since this is your last opportunity to delay or cancel the sale, it's also the best time to pressure the dealer into fixing anything you find wrong with the car. Once you pay for and take delivery on your new car, you won't have as much leverage in getting defects fixed (especially flaws that are cosmetic rather than functional), so your predelivery inspection will be the last important thing you do in the car buying process.

The Predelivery Inspection

As the buyer of a new vehicle, you have the right to one that is free of all defects, from mechanical or functional problems to visual flaws related to "fit and finish." Before you pay for the car and sign the delivery receipt, be sure to perform a thorough inspection of the car, including a road test. If you discover any problems, insist that they be fixed before you take possession.

In order to get you to take delivery (so they can get paid), dealers will usually say, "Don't worry, everything will be fixed to your satisfaction later. All you have to do is bring the car back to our service department, and they'll fix anything that you find wrong. Plus, if you take the car home now, you'll have more time to look it over before you bring it back for servicing." *Don't fall for this.* Insist that they correct all problems before you take possession.

Dealers are usually pretty good about repairing mechanical or functional problems on new cars, but when it comes to cosmetic items like upholstery, paint and other "fit and finish" concerns, they can be very creative in trying to convince you that the flaw you noticed is normal.

You may hear statements like "Oh, that's normal; they all look that way," or my personal favorite, "We can try to make it look better, but it could turn out worse than it is now, then you would have to live with it like that. If I were you, I would leave it alone—it's hardly noticeable." When in doubt, compare with similar new vehicles to see if the situation is normal, then refuse to take delivery if you're not satisfied.

Once you drive away in your new car, any scratches or dents will be assumed to be your fault, so be sure to do a thorough job on the visual inspection—both inside and out. Bring a friend or relative along to double-check for cosmetic flaws, and to help test the accessories and lights.

When you're setting up a time to do the inspection, tell the salesman to leave the "dealer plates" on the car until after you're done with the predelivery inspection and road test. (If he asks why, tell him you want to do the inspection and road test while they still own the car, in case you find something wrong. This might motivate them to make sure the car's in great shape before you get there.)

One last tip: Don't try to do a visual inspection at night. This needs to be done outside, in the sunlight, so make an appointment to do this at your convenience, when the weather is nice. Plan on spending about an hour, less if you have someone to help you.

The following categories should be part of your predelivery inspection:

Serial Number, Mileage & Options. Be sure to check the serial number of the car you picked out against the one on the contract and the one they want you to drive home—they should all be the same. Note the odometer reading; if the car has more than 250-300 miles on it, demand a (believable) explanation. If they can't give you one, tell them to get you another car—that one was probably a "demo" that was loaned to employees for personal use. Confirm that all agreed-upon options are either on the car already or the contract specifies that they are to be installed later. (Don't rely on verbal promises; get everything in writing.)

Body & Paint. Inspect all exterior paint, chrome and trim items for flaws. Look for uneven surfaces, mismatched paint and other evidence of repainting or touch-up, as this could indicate a previously-damaged vehicle that should have been disclosed. (Dealers are required by law to give buyers written disclosure on cars that have had body damage repaired.) Your new car should not have any scratches, dents, or paint flaws—unless you're getting a reduced price to compensate for them.

Minor paint scratches can usually be buffed out, but the car may need repainting if it has deep scratches or other paint flaws. If this is the case, refuse the car and insist that they give you another one. Why? It's almost impossible to repaint part (or all) of a new car and have it look as good as a factory paint job. Even if it does look good immediately after it's repainted, chances are that several years later, after the paint has "aged" in the sun, it won't match perfectly anymore.

Fit and Finish. Inspect the "fit and finish" on all exterior and interior items. The doors, trunk and hood should open and close smoothly and all sheet metal edges should be flush after they are closed. Check the spacing at the sides of the doors and around the trunk and hood—it should be even all the way around. Make sure all movable windows (and sun/moonroof, if equipped) operate smoothly. Check all of the seat belts and seat mechanisms (tracks, motors, recliners, adjustable headrests, etc.) for proper operation. Inspect all upholstery and carpet for defects, poor fit, stains, excess glue, etc. Don't forget to check the headliner (that's the fabric used to cover up the interior side of the roof).

Equipment and Accessories. Have the salesman show you how to operate all of the accessories: lights; stereo; power locks, seats, and windows; air conditioning; cruise control; windshield washers and wipers; rear window defroster; sunroof/moonroof; remote mirrors; security system; etc. Then try them yourself to verify that everything works properly.

This next step involves the help of the friend or relative who came with you. Check all of the lights on the car: headlights, taillights, brake lights, turn signals, emergency flasher, interior and courtesy lights, trunk light, engine compartment light, etc.

Under the Hood. Once again, have the salesman show you how to check all of the fluid levels, where the dipsticks are located, and where to add fluids. Low fluid levels could indicate a leak, or just sloppy new car preparation. Either way, call it to the dealer's attention. If you find several things wrong, tell them to send it back to new car prep for a more thorough job. When you're sure all the fluid levels are OK, do a quick visual check of the tires (all four tires should be the same brand and size, properly inflated), then you're ready for the final phase of the inspection—the road test.

The Road Test. A thorough road test should be done to detect any performance problems related to the engine, transmission, steering and/or brakes. Accelerate quickly from a stop, running through all the gears, then drive at a steady speed. Does the car run smoothly with plenty of power? If it has an automatic transmission, does it shift smoothly?

Take the car through several turns or curves to check the steering and suspension. Does the car handle well? Does it recover quickly after turning? Drive the car at about 30-35 mph on a straight, flat road, then let go of the steering wheel (momentarily). The car should continue traveling in a straight line. If it pulls to one side, the front end alignment should be checked.

Check the brakes under both light and heavy application. The car should stop smoothly and there should be no brake noises or pulsating (unless the car has ABS). On vehicles with Anti-lock Brake Systems, the brake pedal will pulsate during hard braking as the solenoids cycle the hydraulic pressure on and off to prevent wheel lock-up.

To check for squeaks and rattles, drive the car on a bumpy road. Be sure to check the operation of the cruise control and other accessories while driving, and take notes on any problems or noises that were discovered on the road test.

When you're done with the inspection and road test, have the dealer make a copy of your "defect list," then tell him to call you after they've fixed everything on the list. Do another quick inspection to make sure the repairs were done, then check the body and paint to make sure the car didn't get any new dents or scratches while it was in the service department. If everything is OK, you're ready to make your down payment, sign the loan papers and the delivery receipt, then drive home in your new car. Congratulations!

17

Complaints, Lemon Laws & Other Recourse

What can you do if things go wrong with your car, but the dealer can't (or won't) repair it to your satisfaction? Or worse yet, what if your new car is spending more time in the shop than in your driveway, and you're beginning to suspect that it may be a lemon? If it turns out to be a lemon, are you stuck with it?

A number of government agencies exist to help consumers who have disputes with automotive businesses. In addition, numerous independent consumer-advocate groups have sprung up to pressure government agencies to take action on particular issues. These outside groups can also provide valuable information and assistance for consumers who haven't yet found solutions to their automotive problems.

Consumers often have specific rights and protections under the law, but those rights and protections will vary from state to state. For example, there are no federal laws covering "lemons," but all 50 states have their own lemon laws on the books.

Most states also have general "business and professions" laws against deceptive or fraudulent business practices, but only two states (California and Michigan) have separate auto repair agencies to monitor and investigate the shops within their borders.

To find out what specific laws govern the automotive businesses in your state, contact your state attorney general's consumer protection division.

Initial Complaints

The following advice is intended for situations where consumers have no reason to believe that fraud is involved. If you do suspect fraud or other dishonest business practices, contact your local district attorney's office or your state attorney general.

I'm a firm believer that anyone can make an honest mistake, so my advice for consumers regarding their first problem with a business is to immediately voice their complaint with someone in management who has enough authority to handle the problem. In a small business, this may be the owner, but in a large business like a car dealer, you may not be able to speak to the owner. (It's worth a try, though.) The service manager is the head of his department, the sales manager is the top guy for sales, and the general manager is the head of the whole dealership (he reports directly to the owner). Those department heads have authority to resolve difficult problems.

Let's use a repair situation as an example of how to get a problem resolved. You took your car to the dealer's service department to get something repaired, they charged you for it, but it's still not fixed. What do you do?

Remember my initial advice—don't start screaming (yet), and be polite (at least the first time). Give them the benefit of the doubt and a chance to resolve the problem in a way that's fair to you. If the service advisor can arrange this (in a reasonable length of time), let him, but if he starts making excuses, tell him you want to speak to the service manager. Don't accept the service advisor's word as final, especially when you don't think you're being treated fairly.

If the service manager fails to resolve the problem to your satisfaction, then ask for the general manager (or the owner). If no one in the dealership will resolve your problem, ask for the name and phone number of the manufacturer's zone manager.

The zone manager can often find solutions to difficult problems, but don't forget that part of his job is to save the company money. (A cynic would describe the zone manager's job as existing to keep customers as happy as possible, while spending as little of the company's money as possible.) After the zone manager, any further complaints should be sent to the company president.

Be polite, but confident and aggressive. In dealing with all levels of management, let them know that you demand satisfaction and you're not going to give up until you get it. (Remember—"the squeaky wheel gets the grease.") At each step, when you run into roadblocks, always ask for the name and phone number of that person's boss. Let them know you're going to complain to upper management.

Playing Hardball

Threatening to file complaints with government agencies can sometimes be effective, especially if you have a good case against the dealer. (The agencies are listed in this chapter.) However, you may be told, "Go ahead, we don't care." In that case, tell them you're going to write letters to the owner of the dealership *and* the president of the car company, letting them know how unhappy you are with the car and the treatment you received.

Get the names of the managers you dealt with to let them know they will be included in your complaint letters, then ask them for the name and address of the company president so they know you're really going to write. Tell them you're never going to buy another car from their company because of the way you were treated. (Mention one of their competitors who will be getting your future business—they hate hearing that.) Also mention that you're going to be telling everyone you know how badly you were treated, warning them not to buy cars there.

One last tip for extreme cases: Ask the dealer how he would like having you—and your friends—picketing in front of his business every Saturday and Sunday, carrying signs displaying your grievance. (Saturdays and Sundays are the biggest sale days of the week, so that's the best time to picket.) If you have one of those local "action line" TV programs, they might want to get involved, so let the dealer know that you intend to contact them.

Picketing can be very effective in getting problems resolved, but you usually have to follow through on your threat. If you decide to picket, just make sure you stay off the dealer's property—he can have you arrested for trespassing. The sidewalk, however, is usually public property, so that's where to picket. (To be safe, ask the city or county first.) Recruit some friends to help out, bring a picnic lunch, and have fun! Remember, the first amendment guarantees that you have the right to free speech, as long as it's true. If you've struck out at this point, your last resort is to go to court. For minor issues, small claims court can be relatively quick and inexpensive, since no lawyers are allowed in court. For bigger problems, you may need a lawyer. Your local bar association should have a referral service that can set up a low-cost initial consultation with an attorney who specializes in automotive issues. Consumers with good cases can often get attorneys to represent them on a contingency basis. The Center for Auto Safety also offers attorney referrals for lemon law cases.

Mediation and Arbitration

A number of mediation and arbitration programs are also available to help solve consumers' car problems without going to court, but some of them can take months (and months) to reach a conclusion. The national programs usually only handle problems related to factory warranty repairs and defective vehicles (lemons), while some of the local programs may also handle car sales and general repair complaints. Local and state-run arbitration programs seem to be more "consumer-friendly" than national ones, so call your state attorney general's office (and your local Better Business Bureau) to find out if they've set up a program.

If you decide to use arbitration, make sure any decision that is made will only be binding on the manufacturer or dealer, and not on you. A good program will allow the consumer to take his case to court if he doesn't like the final arbitration decision. Check out the program before you make a commitment, and make sure you understand how it works.

Then do your homework: Organize your receipts and repair orders, make an outline of the car's history, and try to locate documents that will back up your case. Write to the Center for Auto Safety for any information they may have on your car, then ask your local dealer and zone manager for any technical service bulletins that mention your particular problem. (You can also get these from the National Highway Traffic Safety Administration.) Include copies of your records and other documents with your application. (Keep the originals.) Request copies of everything submitted by the other side and challenge items you think are incorrect. Don't be afraid to send in additional supporting documents after you've filed your application—just ask that they be included in your file. And be sure to include a copy of your warranty (and your state's lemon law provisions, if applicable).

In the event the arbitrator rules against you, ask how to file an appeal. (You may not be allowed to do this if you've already accepted the decision, so be sure to check out your options before agreeing to anything.) Just because you lost in arbitration doesn't mean you didn't have a good case. After initially losing in arbitration, some consumers have won large judgments against automakers by taking their cases to court.

Lemon Laws

"Lemon laws" are state laws giving consumers specific rights when they have purchased a new car that requires too many repairs within a certain time period. All fifty states have their own lemon laws, but there aren't any federal laws in this area, so specific rules and remedies will vary from state to state. Less than half of the states include leased vehicles in their lemon laws, so be sure to check the laws in your state to see whether your vehicle is covered. The following description is a typical lemon law, but some details may be different in your state.

A new car that is sold with a manufacturer's written warranty may be returned to the manufacturer for a refund (or replacement) if it can't be repaired. 1) The problems must be covered by the warranty and they must substantially reduce the vehicle's safety, value, or use to the consumer. 2) The manufacturer (or its agents) must have made four or more attempts to repair the same problem, or the vehicle must have been out of service for a total of 30 days (not necessarily in a row) while being repaired for any number of problems. 3) The "30 days out of service" or the four repair attempts must have occurred within the first 12 months or 12,000 miles, whichever occurs first. 4) The consumer has directly notified the manufacturer about the problems, if required to do so by the warranty materials or the owner's manual.

If all four of the above conditions exist for a vehicle, a lemon law may presume that the vehicle owner is entitled to a refund or replacement. For manufacturers that provide a certified arbitration program, consumers must first submit their disputes to the program before they are allowed to use the lemon law presumption in a lawsuit against the manufacturer.

To find out how the lemon law works in your state, contact your state attorney general's office or the state department of consumer affairs. You can also write to the Center for Auto Safety.

Auto Repair Tips

Be sure to keep an accurate record of your repair experiences. Take notes. Insist on a written repair order for all repairs, even those done for free under warranty. (You may need those records later to prove that the problem was never really fixed, or that you had too many problems with the same car.) All repair orders should contain the date, mileage and symptom/problem.

Save all receipts and repair orders. Don't allow a shop to keep your only copy of a repair order—make a copy first, then keep the original for yourself. That way you won't find yourself in the helpless position of having no written record of the repairs done to your car.

To avoid being charged for repairs that aren't needed, make sure the initial repair order accurately describes the problem or symptoms you want repaired. If your car's engine dies at stops, don't tell them you want a tune-up, tell them to write up the repair as "diagnose: dies at stops." That way, if they tell you a particular part is causing the problem, and it turns out they're wrong, you'll have written proof that they made a mistake. If necessary, you can use this in small-claims court to get your money back.

Who to Call

NEW & USED CARS

SALES PRACTICES—

Complaints regarding questionable sales practices at new- or used-car dealers should be sent to:

—Local/State Department of Motor Vehicles,
        Bureau of Investigations
—State New Motor Vehicle Board
—Local District Attorney's office
—State Attorney General's office

WARRANTY PROBLEMS, ORIGINAL & EXTENDED—

Complaints regarding a manufacturer's or dealer's failure to honor the original warranty, extended warranty, or service contract should be sent to:

—Manufacturer and/or dealer (by certified mail)
—Local/State Department of Motor Vehicles,
    Bureau of Investigations
—State New Motor Vehicle Board
—Local Consumer Affairs agency

MEDIATION & ARBITRATION—

Better Business Bureau
Auto Line (800) 955-5100

The Better Business Bureau Auto Line provides information on mediation and arbitration services for a number of automakers. Complaints are limited to manufacturers' defects for cars under warranty, although many companies allow a grace period of up to six months.

Your local BBB may also offer mediation and arbitration for disputes with participating dealers and repair shops. They can also record complaints against local businesses and report how complaints have been handled. Contact your local office for details.

STATE-RUN ARBITRATION PROGRAMS—

Over a dozen states have set up their own arbitration programs, and these are usually more "consumer-friendly" than the national ones. To find out if your state has one, contact your state Attorney General's office.

MEDIATION & ARBITRATION—

AUTOCAP
National Automobile Dealers Association
8400 Westpark Drive
McLean, VA 22102
(703) 821-7144

AUTOCAP provides third-party mediation for sales and service problems with manufacturers or dealers. Arbitration is also available for unresolved problems.

Note: Since AUTOCAP is a voluntary program run by state and local dealer associations, some dealers may not participate. In addition, many AUTOCAP programs do not follow the arbitration guidelines required for warranty cases by the FTC.

LEMON LAWS, SECRET WARRANTIES, VEHICLE DEFECTS, SAFETY RECALLS—

Center for Auto Safety
2001 S Street NW, Suite 410
Washington, DC 20009
(202) 328-7700

The Center for Auto Safety is a non-profit clearing house for information on lemon laws, secret warranties, vehicle defects, recalls and attorney referral to lemon law specialists. To receive information, send a self-addressed, stamped envelope to the Center with a note listing the year, make and model of your vehicle. Don't forget to specify what kind of information you need. (Normal response time is 3-4 weeks.)

FACTORY RECALLS, SAFETY DEFECTS & SERVICE BULLETINS—

National Highway Traffic Safety Administration
400 7th Street SW, Room 5110
Washington, DC 20590
Auto Safety Hotline (800) 424-9393

NHTSA collects information on all automotive recalls (including child safety seats), safety defects and complaints, crash tests, standards for all automotive parts, and factory service bulletins covering all vehicles sold in the United States. For a fee, they will research service bulletins to locate those explaining a manufacturer's solution to a difficult repair problem. They also have certified data and films on crash tests. **Be sure to notify NHTSA if you discover a manufacturer's defect that could impair the safety of your vehicle.**

For GM, FORD and VW vehicles, information on factory service bulletins can also be obtained by calling the following manufacturers' toll-free customer service numbers:
GM (800) 551-4123; FORD (800) 241-3673;
VW (800) 544-8021.

If you need to get recall or service bulletin information immediately, any repair shop with an Alldata computerized information system can print them out for you (typical charge: $10-15). To locate a shop near you, call Alldata Corp. at (800) 829-8727, select "operator."

VEHICLE DEFECTS, CONSUMER COMPLAINTS & ARBITRATION INFO—

Federal Trade Commission
6th & Pennsylvania Avenue, NW
Washington, DC 20580
(202) 326-2000

The FTC investigates unfair or deceptive trade practices in the sale and repair of automobiles. Complaints regarding these practices should be filed with the Commission. The FTC also collects information and complaints regarding vehicle defects, which can be used to force automakers to offer free repairs for common problems. Information on arbitration is also available.

EMISSION WARRANTIES—

Environmental Protection Agency
1200 Pennsylvania Ave NW
Washington, DC 20460
(202) 260-2090

The EPA has complete information on all vehicle emission warranties, gas mileage data for all vehicles, and import/export emission information.

AUTO REPAIR COMPLAINTS

CALIFORNIA—
Bureau of Automotive Repair
10240 Systems Parkway
Sacramento, CA 95827
Calif. only (800) 952-5210
All others (916) 445-1254

MICHIGAN—
Bureau of Automotive Regulation
208 N. Capitol Ave.
Lansing, MI 48918
Mich. only (800) 292-4204
All others   (517) 373-7416

ALL OTHER STATES—
Contact your state Consumer Protection Agency,
or the state Attorney General's office

For complaints against auto repair shops, call or write the appropriate agency for your state. Complaint forms can usually be requested by phone. Action can be taken for obvious violations of a state's laws or regulations. If numerous complaints are filed against one shop, an investigation may be started.

Complaints can also be made to your local Better Business Bureau and city/county District Attorney's consumer protection division.

18

Tips for Used-Car Buyers

Buying a good late-model, low-mileage, used car instead of a new one can go a long way toward keeping your driving costs down. For owners of new cars, the biggest expense is depreciation, with a car suffering its biggest drop in value during the first 2-3 years. So, let the first owner pay for that, then step in and buy the car at a big discount from its original price.

Previous lease vehicles can offer great value for a low price. The market value of a low-mileage, 2- or 3-year-old off-lease vehicle will be about 35-50% below original retail even though it's still in excellent condition. It will cost a lot less over time to drive one of these compared to a brand-new model, especially if the used car is kept at least 3-4 years.

To avoid paying too much for a used car or truck, be

sure to check several local newspapers to compare prices on similar vehicles. Most bookstores and libraries carry inexpensive used-car price guides (see Chapter 11), but those are merely estimates. The actual market value of a particular vehicle is determined by what people are willing to pay for similar cars in your area.

When buying from a private party, you'll be buying the vehicle "as is" (unless it's still under the original warranty). This means no warranty at all. So, if you're not an experienced auto mechanic, don't ever buy a used car without having *your* mechanic give it a thorough inspection before you sign any contracts or pay any money. You'll have to pay for the inspection, but it's money well-spent, and any problems that are discovered can often be used to negotiate a lower price.

Be wary of verbal promises. Non-written statements concerning a car's condition (or warranty) are almost always worthless. *If someone won't put it in writing, it's probably not true.*

Buying From a Dealer

If you are considering the purchase of a used vehicle from a car dealer, keep in mind that many dealers make more money on a used car than a new one, simply because it's much easier for consumers to find out what the dealer's cost is on a new car. The higher the price, the bigger the profit margin, so don't be afraid to offer a lot less than the asking price. It's not unusual for a dealer to make $2,000 to $3,000 profit on a used car selling for $10,000 so there's plenty of room to negotiate.

Most dealers sell their used cars "as is" (without any warranty), and they're not usually very cooperative when it comes to letting people take their vehicles to other shops for prepurchase inspections. Of course, they'll have lots of excuses for those policies. Here are several examples (which are often untrue): "That's not necessary, our mechanics have already done a thorough inspection." "All of our cars are completely safety-checked. They wouldn't be on our lot if they needed any repairs."

While it may be true that a dealer's cars have been "safety-checked" so you're not going to have a steering or brake failure on the way home from the dealer, I seriously doubt that their inspections are very thorough, or done with full disclosure. I've heard too many horror stories from used-car buyers to believe otherwise.

Negotiating Tactics

You can take advantage of a dealer's reluctance to have his cars inspected by insisting on a free warranty. Even though all used cars on a dealer's lot may be marked "as is," don't forget that practically everything is negotiable when you're buying a car. Just say, "If the car's condition is as good as you say, you shouldn't have any problem giving me a written, bumper-to-bumper six-month warranty." (Ask for six months, settle for three if that's the best deal you can get.)

At this point, the salesman will probably say that they can't do that (which isn't usually true) and counter with a suggestion that you should buy an extended warranty (for $1,000 to $1,500) if you're so concerned with future repair costs. Extended warranties are negotiable, and they only cost the dealer 30-50% of the amount most people pay for them, so tell the salesman he's going to have to throw in the warranty or you're not going to buy the car.

Here's where you use your "best negotiating weapon" if he says he can't give you any kind of warranty—tell him you're going to find another dealer who's more cooperative, then leave. If he really wants to sell you a car, he'll stop you. Don't compromise on your first visit—tell him to throw in the warranty, or you're leaving.

If you've done your homework so you know what the car's really worth, and the amount you're offering to pay is far below the dealer's asking price, there may not be enough profit in the deal for the dealer to pay the whole cost of the extended warranty. In that case, you might have to increase your offer, or pay for the warranty yourself. Be wary of offers to "split the cost of the warranty," because the dealer could double the price so you end up paying the whole cost. (Buy an MBI policy instead.)

Factory "Certified Vehicle" Programs

Most of the automakers are now operating "certified vehicle" programs to help dealers compete with the used-car superstores—and prop up used-car prices. Select low-mileage vehicles that are put through an inspection and reconditioning program are then given an extended factory warranty with coverage ranging from 1 year/12,000 miles to 6 years/100,000 miles. This extra coverage is usually included in the higher prices that are put on these vehicles, so do your homework and be sure to negotiate.

Final Tips

Research market values before you go shopping. Unless a dealer lets you get a prepurchase inspection, don't buy a used car from him without some kind of free written warranty. Remember to "make an offer, then walk out" to get the best deal. If you're buying a used car from a private party, make sure you have *your* mechanic check the car thoroughly *before* you buy it. And if having an extended warranty would help you to sleep at night, be sure to get a good one at a discount price. (See Chapter 6.)

19

Dealers & The Media: Blackmail or Censorship?

Why are most consumers unaware of the dirty tricks that many car dealers have been using to overcharge (and cheat) their customers? Is it because few people know the inside secrets and fewer still are willing to tell the public what they know? Or is it because a serious effort is made to prevent the truth from getting out?

An article I found in the April '92 issue of *Consumer Reports* suggests that the last question is closer to the truth. The article was titled, "Are automobile dealers editing your local newspaper?" and it details the pressure car dealers often put on newspapers to keep them from printing anything dealers may consider "unfavorable."

The *Consumer Reports* article gave specific examples of newspapers that printed wire-service stories on how to bargain when buying a car. A barrage of car dealer complaints on the "lucky" newspapers resulted in an unofficial policy to avoid similar articles in the future. The unlucky newspapers were punished by car dealers who pulled their ads; some papers lost all of their auto advertising for up to six months, until the papers apologized for running the "offending" stories.

Were these just a few isolated incidents, or examples of common practices in the media? To find out, *Consumer Reports* conducted a random survey of 50 daily newspapers, asking editors and writers if local car dealers had any effect on the news. About one-third of the journalists in the survey admitted that they wouldn't run stories on car buying due to actual (or anticipated) dealer complaints.

One syndicated columnist told me that any articles on "how to save money when buying a new car" would only be printed in 50-60% of the papers carrying the column. Another columnist said that any articles car dealers might see as "unfriendly" had to be very carefully worded or most papers wouldn't print them.

The following story is a perfect illustration of the "dealers vs. the media" problem.

1994: Dealers vs. the *San Jose Mercury News*

On May 22, 1994 the *San Jose Mercury News* (a major newspaper in the San Francisco Bay area) ran a story titled, "A Car Buyer's Guide to Sanity." The article gave readers tips on how to negotiate lower prices with car dealers and included information on how to find out what the dealer's cost was on a particular model. A specific car buying service was also mentioned, with an explanation of how they force dealers to bid against each other, a process designed to get the lowest possible price. (The two services that received the best reviews in the article were Fighting Chance and CarBargains, both recommended by me in this book.)

The next day, local dealers complained about the article, so a meeting between the publisher and about three dozen dealers was set for May 25. According to the executive editor of the *Mercury News*, the dealers were upset by the "tone" of the article, citing three "offensive" quotes that were printed. One quote came from the president of the car buying service, who said that the "real power of information is that it keeps the dealers honest." Another quote came from the founder and president of Fighting Chance, who said, "One reason God gave you feet was so you could use them to walk away from car salesmen." *That one is my personal favorite.*

According to the president of the local dealers' association, dealers were insulted by the tone of the article, claiming they were portrayed as being unethical. One dealer claimed that the article said they take advantage of people. *I'm sure that's never happened!*

At the meeting, the publisher was reported to have defended the article and the reporter who wrote it. Several weeks later, over 40 dealers pulled their advertising from the paper, saying they were upset with the arrogant attitude of the *Mercury News*. (What nerve that paper had, deciding what to print without asking their advertisers first. Who do they think they are, anyway?)

Local dealers denied that the cancelled ads were part of a coordinated effort, but the newspaper got the message, nonetheless. (Estimates of lost advertising revenue were at least $1 million.) Newspaper officials took steps to patch things up with the dealers, publishing follow-up stories that implied that the (offending) article was not well-written. They also ran a full-page color ad promoting area dealers, encouraging readers to purchase cars from them.

The fence-mending efforts of the *Mercury News* paid off. By July, some of the dealers had returned as advertisers and more were expected within the next few months. According to the president of the dealers' association, they returned because of the paper's efforts to mend relations with the dealers and, ironically, *because they had no other viable alternative for advertising.* (The cancelled ads probably hurt the dealers more than the newspaper.)

Due to the actions taken by newspaper officials, fellow reporters felt that the writer had been discredited. They also were concerned that it looked like the newspaper had caved in to pressure from advertisers. *No, not at all!* The writer also said he would think twice before covering another auto topic.

Enter the Federal Trade Commission

After a story about the *Mercury News* situation appeared in the *Washington Post*, the Federal Trade Commission opened an investigation to determine whether the local car dealers violated federal laws that prohibit anticompetitive agreements. The FTC was particularly interested in a dealer meeting held at the San Jose Hyatt Hotel shortly after dealers met with *Mercury News* officials. (Advertising cancellations started soon after the dealer meeting.)

The issue: When the dealers pulled their advertising, were they (in effect) agreeing not to compete, and did their actions depress competition in the local area? The FTC was not challenging the right of dealers to stop advertising, or to punish newspapers for running articles they dislike. Whether actions were taken that restricted competition was the issue.

The president of the local dealers' association denied that the dealers acted together in pulling their ads. *I'm sure it was just a coincidence.*

In an unrelated case, the FTC completed an investigation of the Arizona Automobile Dealers Association regarding possible antitrust violations in 1994. Without admitting guilt, the association signed a consent agreement that promised to eliminate restrictions that prohibited discount advertising. The association represented about 99% of the new car and truck dealers in that state and they had a "Standards for Advertising Motor Vehicles" policy that prohibited ads such as "we'll beat any price."

1995: Dealers vs. Buffalo TV Station?

On February 15, 1995 ABC's *PrimeTime Live* aired a show on new-car leasing scams, using hidden cameras and a female reporter posing as a customer. In the show, *PrimeTime* accused a number of dealers of trying to overcharge on leases. (See Chapter 1 for details of the show.)

According to a February 20 story in *USA Today*, one station (WKBW in Buffalo, New York) preempted the *PrimeTime* auto leasing show. One hour of *Roseanne* reruns was aired instead. The article said, "Word around ABC News is that local car dealers pressured the station to yank the show for the night."

1996-98: Blackmail, Censorship or News Coverup?

The most glaring examples of the news media failing to cover consumer protection stories about their advertisers occurred between 1996 and late 1998. First, five new-car dealers in Sacramento (California) were accused of cheating people on leases following an investigation by local prosecutors. To settle the charges, the dealers agreed to

187

pay civil penalties and to make restitution to 111 people. This story got no press or TV news coverage, even though at least one TV station had been working on it. Sources claim that the dealers were able to get the story killed—*because they were major advertisers.*

In 1997, I exposed a major automaker's involvement in widespread leasing rip-offs by its dealers, first in a book *(Leasing Lessons for Smart Shoppers),* then on the Internet. My exposé was followed by a state prosecutor's public announcement that 22 states were conducting investigations into the leasing practices of the same automaker (and its dealers), but major newspapers and TV news organizations failed to cover the story.

In fact, a major TV newsmagazine had been working on this leasing story and was supposedly close to airing it several times. However, in spite of the fact that their own people had fact-checked the whole story in preparation for broadcast (they said it was "a solid piece" and "a big story"), management killed it. They said the decision to kill the piece had nothing to do with the fact that the target was a major advertiser. (That automaker and its dealers spend over a billion dollars a year on ads, many of which air on that network and its local stations.)

Several large, "respectable" newspapers were also supposed to cover this leasing story, but they never did. They also claimed that the lack of coverage was unrelated to the subject being a major advertiser.

It should be obvious by now why it's so easy for dishonest car dealers to victimize so many people: A lot of consumer protection information has been kept out of the mainstream media because management did not want to upset their advertisers. And there have already been many attempts to keep the secrets in this book from getting out, so do your friends a favor and tell them about this book.

Summary

By now, you've probably learned more than you ever wanted to know about the new-car business. And even if you only skimmed through the book, you know a lot more than most dealers would like. But don't assume that all dealers and salesmen are dishonest, because they're not. I just exposed all the dirty tricks so you can tell the good guys from the bad. When you do find an honest dealer, tell all your friends—they'll appreciate it, and so will the dealer.

The secret to getting the best price is competition based on information. Find out how big the profit margin is on a car, then make the dealers compete against each other so you end up with the lowest possible price. When you're done, you'll know you got a good deal.

Don't get into arguments over how much profit a dealer "should make," that's for him to decide, not you or me, not the car manufacturers, not the government. I just thought you should know that dealers do sell cars at huge discounts that aren't advertised—*they just don't want you to know.*

And don't feel bad if a dealer only makes a small profit on your car. Chances are the next customer (who hasn't read this book) will more than make up for it.

Appendix

Worksheet #1 — Lease Information

Vehicle year, make, model _____

Retail price (MSRP) _____

Vehicle Price:

A. Negotiated vehicle price _____

B. Add-ons: (warranty, insurance, etc.)

_____

C. <u>Gross cap cost</u> (A+B)   _____

Credits:

D. Cash down payment   _____

E. Net trade-in allowance _____

F. Rebates   _____

G. <u>Total cap cost reduction</u> (D+E+F)   _____

Lease Terms:

<u>Net cap cost</u> (C minus G)   _____

Term _____ Money factor _____ Interest rate _____

Monthly payment _____ Residual value _____

H. <u>Total of monthly payments</u>   _____

Amounts due at lease signing:

Cash down payment (optional)   _____

Net trade-in allowance (optional)   _____

Refundable security deposit   _____

1) Acquisition fee   _____

2) Title/registration fees   _____

3) Sales tax on cap reduction (G)   _____

First month's payment   _____

<u>Total due at lease signing</u>   _____

Total cost of lease (G+H+1+2+3)   _____

Worksheet #2 — Lease Payment Calculation

Part 1: Monthly Depreciation
[Term is the length of the lease in months.]
Monthly Depreciation =
  (Net Cap Cost — Residual) ÷ Term

Net Cap Cost   _____
Minus Residual   _____
Total   _____
÷ Term   _____
Monthly Depreciation _____

Part 2: Lease Rate (Monthly Finance Charge)
Money Factor = APR [.xxx] ÷ 24
Lease Rate = (Net Cap Cost + Residual) X Money Factor

Net Cap Cost   _____
Plus Residual   _____
Total   _____
Times Money Factor   _____
Monthly Lease Rate   _____

Part 3: Total Monthly Payment
Monthly Payment = Monthly Depreciation + Lease Rate
(Plus applicable sales tax on the total monthly payment)

Monthly Depreciation   _____
Plus Monthly Lease Rate   _____
Monthly Payment   _____
(Plus Sales Tax)   _____
(Monthly Payment w/Tax)   _____

Worksheet #3 — Purchase Information

Vehicle year, make, model _____

Retail price (MSRP) _____

Vehicle Price:

A. Negotiated vehicle price _____

B. Add-ons: (warranty, insurance, etc.)

_____

C. Total purchase price (A+B)   _____

Credits:

D. Cash down payment   _____

E. Net trade-in allowance _____

F. Rebates   _____

G. Total credits (D+E+F)   _____

Financing:

Loan amount (C minus G)   _____

Term _____ Interest rate _____

Monthly payment _____

H. Total of monthly payments   _____

Amounts due at loan signing:

Cash down payment (optional)   _____

Net trade-in allowance (optional)   _____

1) Title/registration fees   _____

2) Sales tax   _____

Total due at loan signing .   _____

Total cost of purchase (G+H+1+2)   _____

Minus equity at end of term   _____

Net cost of purchase   _____

Payment Tables

The following tables of lease and loan payments are provided for educational purposes; they are not meant to cover all possible lease or loan situations.

Your actual payments may vary, depending on the negotiated price, down payment, trade-in, rebate, interest rate, residual, and length of lease (or loan). Since the possible combinations of factors are virtually unlimited, it would not be practical to attempt listing them in print.

To calculate the monthly payments for combinations not listed here, use the preceding worksheets and the procedure outlined under "How to Figure Lease Payments" in Chapter 2. Or you can use the computer program I used: "Expert Lease Pro" by CHART Software. (See Chapter 11, "Homework for Car Buyers," for more information on this program.)

Table 1

LEASE

Monthly Lease Payments
$10,000 to $25,000 Cap Cost (Price)
8% APR, 0 Down

Cap Cost	24 mos.	36 mos.	48 mos.
10,000	219	189	172
11,000	241	208	189
12,000	263	227	206
13,000	285	245	224
14,000	307	264	241
15,000	329	283	258
16,000	351	302	275
17,000	373	321	292
18,000	395	340	310
19,000	417	359	327
20,000	439	378	344
21,000	461	396	361
22,000	483	415	378
23,000	505	434	396
24,000	527	453	413
25,000	549	472	430

(Amounts rounded to nearest dollar.)
Residuals: 60% (24 mos.), 50% (36 mos.), 40% (48 mos.)

Table 2

PURCHASE

Monthly Loan Payments
$10,000 to $25,000 Loan Amounts
8% APR

Loan Amount	36 mos.	48 mos.	60 mos.
10,000	313	244	203
11,000	345	269	223
12,000	376	293	243
13,000	407	317	264
14,000	439	342	284
15,000	470	366	304
16,000	501	391	324
17,000	533	415	345
18,000	564	439	365
19,000	595	464	385
20,000	627	488	406
21,000	658	513	426
22,000	689	537	446
23,000	721	562	466
24,000	752	586	487
25,000	783	610	507

(Amounts rounded to nearest dollar.)

Table 3

LEASE

Monthly Lease Payments
Based on APR Changes
$20,000 Cap Cost (Price)
7% to 12% APR, 0 Down

APR	24 mos.	36 mos.	48 mos.
7%	426	365	332
8%	439	378	344
9%	452	390	356
10%	465	403	368
11%	478	415	380
12%	492	428	392

(Amounts rounded to nearest dollar.)
Residuals: 60% (24 mos.), 50% (36 mos.), 40% (48 mos.)

Table 4

PURCHASE

Monthly Loan Payments
Based on APR Changes
$20,000 Loan Amount
7% to 12% APR

APR	36 mos.	48 mos.	60 mos.
7%	618	479	396
8%	627	488	406
9%	636	498	415
10%	645	507	425
11%	655	517	435
12%	664	527	445

(Amounts rounded to nearest dollar.)

Table 5

PURCHASE

Monthly Loan Payments
$10,000 to $25,000 Loan Amounts
7% to 12% APR
36 months

Loan Amount	7%	8%	9%	10%	11%	12%
10,000	309	313	318	323	327	332
11,000	340	345	350	355	360	365
12,000	371	376	382	387	393	399
13,000	401	407	413	419	426	432
14,000	432	439	445	452	458	465
15,000	463	470	477	484	491	498
16,000	494	501	509	516	524	531
17,000	525	533	541	549	557	565
18,000	556	564	572	581	589	598
19,000	587	595	604	613	622	631
20,000	618	627	636	645	655	664
21,000	648	658	668	678	688	698
22,000	679	689	700	710	720	731
23,000	710	721	731	742	753	764
24,000	741	752	763	774	786	797
25,000	772	783	795	807	818	830

(Amounts rounded to nearest dollar.)

Table 6

PURCHASE

Monthly Loan Payments
$10,000 to $25,000 Loan Amounts
7% to 12% APR
48 months

Loan Amount	7%	8%	9%	10%	11%	12%
10,000	239	244	249	254	258	263
11,000	263	269	274	279	284	290
12,000	287	293	299	304	310	316
13,000	311	317	324	330	336	342
14,000	335	342	348	355	362	369
15,000	359	366	373	380	388	395
16,000	383	391	398	406	414	421
17,000	407	415	423	431	439	448
18,000	431	439	448	457	465	474
19,000	455	464	473	482	491	500
20,000	479	488	498	507	517	527
21,000	503	513	523	533	543	553
22,000	527	537	547	558	569	579
23,000	551	562	572	583	594	606
24,000	575	586	597	609	620	632
25,000	599	610	622	634	646	658

(Amounts rounded to nearest dollar.)

Table 7

PURCHASE

Monthly Loan Payments
$10,000 to $25,000 Loan Amounts
7% to 12% APR
60 months

Loan Amount	7%	8%	9%	10%	11%	12%
10,000	198	203	208	212	217	222
11,000	218	223	228	234	239	245
12,000	238	243	249	255	261	267
13,000	257	264	270	276	283	289
14,000	277	284	291	297	304	311
15,000	297	304	311	319	326	334
16,000	317	324	332	340	348	356
17,000	337	345	353	361	370	378
18,000	356	365	374	382	391	400
19,000	376	385	394	404	413	423
20,000	396	406	415	425	435	445
21,000	416	426	436	446	457	467
22,000	436	446	457	467	478	489
23,000	455	466	477	489	500	512
24,000	475	487	498	510	522	534
25,000	495	507	519	531	544	556

(Amounts rounded to nearest dollar.)

Another consumer book by

Mark Eskeldson

What Auto Mechanics Don't Want You to Know

LEARN ALL ABOUT:

Secret Warranties:
How to Get Free Repairs

Undercover Investigations:
Well-Known Repair Shops That Have Been Busted

Avoiding Repair Scams;
Getting Your Money Back

Finding Mechanics You Can Trust

Vehicle Maintenance Secrets

"...a better-informed consumer is less likely to be taken
advantage of. And that's why Eskeldson wrote his
book...Even if you don't have the time to spend reading...keep the book as a reference."
—*CAR AND DRIVER*

Technews Publishing, $12.95
ISBN 0-9640560-6-2

Both books available in bookstores
or call (800) 528-8634
All orders shipped within 5 days
Money-back Guarantee

Another consumer book by

Mark Eskeldson

Leasing Lessons
for Smart Shoppers

Company Secrets Revealed
From Documents & Training Manuals

FIND OUT

How Salespeople Were Trained
To Cheat Customers

Why Down Payments On Leases
Are Usually a Big Mistake

How Much Lease Payments Should Be

Everything You Need to Know
To Get a Great Deal

$8.95 plus s&h

To order, call 1-800-528-8634